North Country Gardening
with Wildflowers

Other Books by Neil Moran
North Country Gardening: Simple Secrets to Successful Northern Gardening
From Store to Garden: 101 Ways to Make the Most of Garden Store Purchases

North Country Gardening with Wildflowers

A Guide to Growing and Enjoying Native Plants in the Upper Great Lakes Region

by Neil Moran

Illustrations by
Patrick Rambo

Haylake Publishing
Sault Ste. Marie, MI

North Country Gardening with Wildflowers by Neil Moran
Copyright © 2011 Neil Moran. All Rights Reserved
Illustrations by Patrick Rambo
Copyright © 2011 Patrick Rambo. Used by permission.

No portion of this book may be be copied, reproduced, or transmitt ed in any form or by any means, electronic or otherwise, including recording, photocopying, or inclusion in any information storage and retrieval system, without the express written permission of the author, except for brief exerpts quoted in published reviews.

Book and cover design by Five Rainbows Services www.FiveRainbows.com

First Edition
Manufactured in the United States.

Haylake Publishing
www.NeilMoran.com

Publisher's Cataloging-in-Publication Data

Moran, Neil.
    North country gardening with wildflowers : a guide to growing and enjoying native plants in the upper Great Lakes region / Neil Moran ; illustrations by Patrick Rambo.
        p. cm.
   ISBN: 978-0-9834413-0-4
   1. Wild flower gardening—Middle West. 2. Native plant gardening—Michigan. 3. Gardening—Michigan—Upper Peninsula.   I. Rambo, Patrick, ill. II. Title.
SB453.2.M525 M67 2011
635`.09774—dc22

                                                        2011925296

WILDFLOWER IDENTIFICATION
FOR FRONT COVER PHOTO

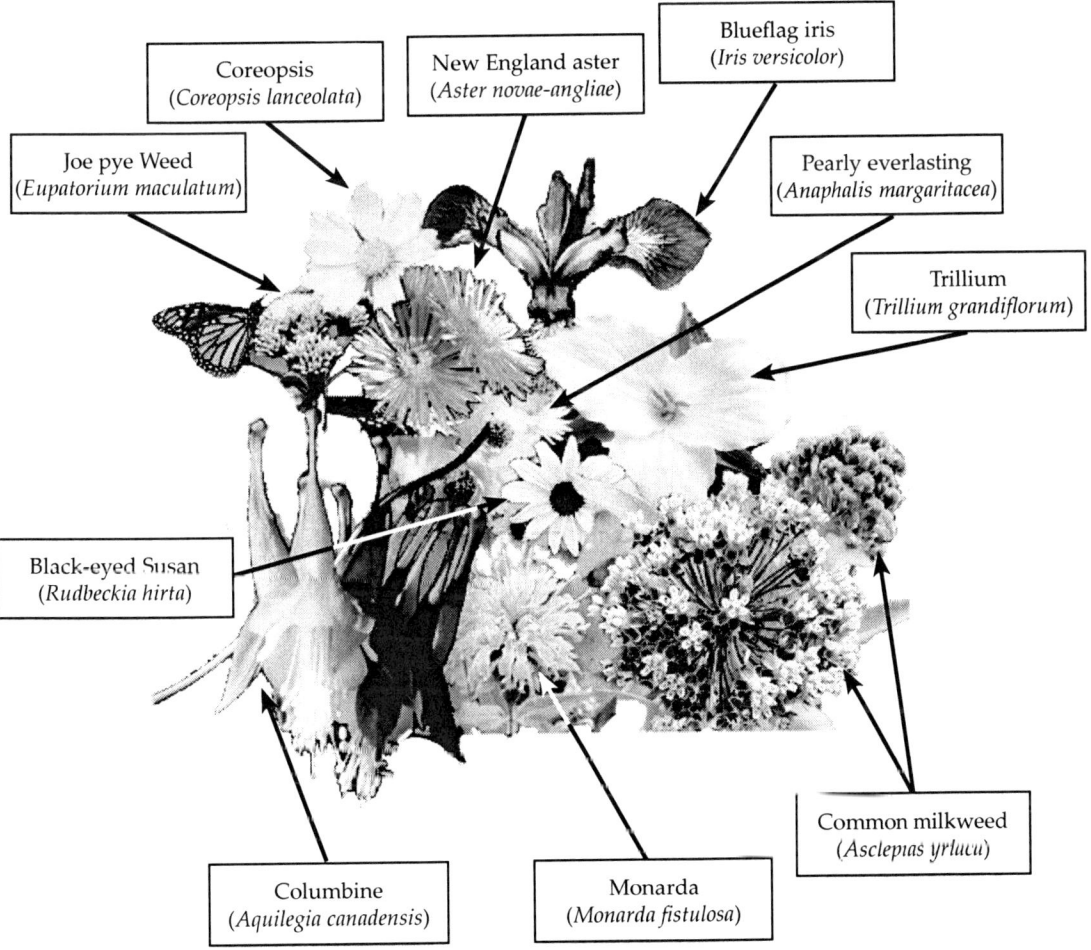

This book is dedicated to all the people who work to preserve the natural world.

Acknowledgments

Like any endeavor of this magnitude, this book couldn't have been written without the help and support of other folks. I owe a debt of gratitude to my wife, Sherri, for her continued support and encouragement. I also owe thanks to fellow board members of the Northern Wild Plant and Seed Cooperative: Karen Bartunek, Dusty King, and Wendy Wagoner for the financial backing for this project and also all of the resources and information they have given me, taken from their many years of involvement and love for wildflowers and nature in general. Their advice on changes the days before I wrapped up this project were invaluable. Quite frankly, I couldn't have asked for a better group to collaborate on such a project. Finally, I thank Patrick Rambo, who was a student at the Sault Area Middle School in Sault Ste. Marie, Michigan, at the time this book went to print, for all of the wonderful drawings done of the plant species featured in Chapter 5 of this book. He was a pleasure to work with and I'm sure he'll go on to do great things.

CONTENTS

      Chapter 1—Is This Book for Me?
      Chapter 2—Introduction to the Benefits of Wildflowers
      Chapter 3—Taking to the Woods and Fields: Seed Collection
      Chapter 4—Seed Germination Secrets Revealed
19   Chapter 5—Starting Selected Wildflowers from Seed
59   Chapter 6—Other Plant Propagation Methods
65   Chapter 7—A Few Tips on Soil
69   Chapter 8—Creating a Wildlife Oasis
73   Chapter 9—Keep It Natural: Landscaping with Wildflowers
85   Chapter 10—A Rain Garden of Wildflowers
91   Chapter 11—Be on the Lookout for Invasive Species!
97   Glossary: For Your Understanding
103 Appendix A: More Information & Resources
109 Appendix B: Books, Hikes & More
117 About the Author

1

S THIS BOOK FOR ME?

If you've ever wanted to establish a native prairie or meadow, or just incorporate a few native plants into your yard or garden, this book is for you. Other folks who may be interested in this book include wildflower groups, government agencies, and groups devoted to preserving our natural surroundings, such as the U.S. Forest Service, soil conservation districts, the Wild Ones, and the Nature Conservancy. These groups engage in projects such as dune restoration and restoring other neglected or abused sites to their original native splendor. This will be a valuable handbook for acquiring detailed information on seed collection, propagation, site preparation, and maintenance of a wildflower planting.

Much of the trial and error of starting native plants by seed or vegetative propagation has been done for you and detailed in this book. Although it's not an exhaustive book in terms of including every single native plant you may encounter or wish to plant, I have tried to include a pretty wide range of native plants, especially those that are popular and useful in various situations and soil conditions, including upland, swamp, clay, and sandy sites. I think you will also find there is a common thread in the propagation of most species of native wildflowers; that is, experiment, experiment, experiment!

And finally, this book is for people who just plain enjoy seeking out native plants on their excursions throughout the Upper Great Lakes region. That's why

North Country Gardening with Wildflowers

I have included a list of some native plant hot spots in this region. I've listed some of the managed "natural areas" near the cities, but also what I feel is the real McCoy of wilderness areas for viewing wildflowers—places such as the Seney Wildlife Refuge, in Michigan's Upper Peninsula, Whitewater State Park in southeastern Minnesota, and Peninsula State Park, in Wisconsin's Door County.

It is my hope that this book will be a springboard for both your enjoyment and propagation of native plants. In a natural world that is constantly shrinking due to over development, I think you will find, upon reading this book, that we can do our part to keep the natural world natural, if only in our own backyards.

Karen Bartunek enjoys some beautiful New England asters in her garden of wildflowers.

2

Introduction to the Benefits of Wildflowers

Karen Bartunek of Dafter, Michigan, grows native plants to attract beneficial insects that will help control pests in her greenhouse and gardens. Dusty King, of Barbeau, Michigan, uses native plants to create a buffer zone to halt potentially harmful runoff into the river that lies near her waterfront cottage.

Wendy Wagoner, of Cedarville, Michigan, uses native plants for medicinal purposes and to attract critters to her property—critters such as ruby-throated hummingbirds and monarch butterflies.

And finally, a number of agencies, departments and conservation groups rely on native plants for various projects including reestablishing dunes around the Great Lakes region, restoring wetland habitats, and filling in cleared areas (such as utility right-of-ways) with native plants.

In 2001, I joined the Northern Wild Plant and Seed Co-op, a fledgling group of native-plant enthusiasts in Chippewa County, in Michigan's Upper Peninsula. Over the years we have seen slow but steady interest in growing and enjoying plants native to this region. However, it is evident that growing native plants has not caught on in some parts of the North quite like it has in other areas of the country. Perhaps this is because our woods are still vast and people think there is no need for growing plants that occur here naturally.

The fact is, we're seeing more development in all areas in the Great Lakes region. Well-meaning folks are building houses in wooded areas, on the banks of the rivers, and overlooking our beautiful lakes. Development of our wild areas poses potential problems for the environment, such as loss of native habitat, pesticides seeping into our water sources, and the introduction of invasive species of plants that not only push out native plants, but offer little benefit for local wildlife.

Once established, wildflowers require far less watering than grass and most ornamental landscape plants.

Each year I've questioned myself on why I would spend two hours on a lawn mower each week cutting grass and polluting the environment when I could be working in my garden growing food for my family, or heck, maybe just relaxing on the deck! Over the past few years, I've managed to wean myself away more and more from this time-honored but questionable tradition. I've established swathes of native plants in several areas of my yard, a strategy which has cut my mowing time in half.

Folks are starting to see the futility of maintaining the "perfect lawn." They are starting to realize the harm to the environment that is caused from a season-long drenching of chemical fertilizers and herbicides (some provinces in Canada are even banning herbicides), not to mention the pollution lawn mowers emit. According to some accounts, a family mowing one-third of an acre of lawn applies the equivalent of 7 gallons of petroleum annually just to fertilize their lawn. In addition, we Americans will burn through 600 million gallons of gas mowing and trimming our lawns each year. More and more folks are opting to turn all or a portion of their lawn into vegetable and flower gardens, ponds, or a wildflower oasis resembling a meadow or a wind-blown prairie. Change is hard. But the more you see the benefit of less lawn and more native plants, the more likely you will be to make the switch to a more natural landscape.

These gardeners are stocking up on native plants at the Prairie Nursery in Westfield, Wisconsin.

This is an opportune time to learn about native plants, and more importantly, to grow them around our homes, our businesses, and in our wild areas. This is not to say that native wildflowers should replace the beautiful horticultural plants that we have come to love (I love geraniums as much as anyone!). It is more about learning how important native plants are to our environment and what they can do for us, such as attract the wildlife that we have come to appreciate here in the North.

Seldom can you pick up a newspaper these days without reading about climate change, invasive species, and threats to honeybees. Fortunately, there is something we can do about these problems—perhaps in a small way—while enhancing our own landscapes and enjoying the beauty of native plants.

Growing native plants will help combat the steady march of invasive species into our wild areas. By learning more about native plants, we will come to understand the threat of invasive species. We will see that we need native plants to help achieve and maintain an ecological balance.

Wendy Wagoner examines some beneficial grasses.

Plants of any kind take up carbon dioxide, the gas that some scientists believe is responsible for global warming. The more native plants we grow, the more carbon dioxide will be removed from the atmosphere, which will help fight global warming.

And lastly, honeybees are under attack—possibly by man-made influences, such as, pesticide usage, resulting in a phenomenon called colony collapse disorder (CCD). Needless to say, we need insect pollination to grow the fruit that feeds the world (unless we don't mind a steady diet of oatmeal!). Native plants will attract other insect pollinators that will do the job that we have come to rely on nonnative honeybees to do.

Furthermore, native plants;
- flourish without fertilizers or synthetic pesticides;
- rarely need watering;
- provide food and habitat for wildlife;
- contribute to biodiversity;
- connect us to our natural surroundings, our natural history, and—by their very nature—help us celebrate the things that make our region unique;
- and lastly, by gosh, they're beautiful!

Native plants keep us in tune with the natural world. Native plants, and gardening in general, help to keep us grounded in this otherwise fast-paced world, or in the words of Ralph Waldo Emerson, "adopt the pace of nature: her secret is patience."

To understand native plants is to understand nature herself. Growing and enjoying native plants serve as subtle reminders of how we need clean water, clean air, and the wildlife that surrounds us, so that we can all live and grow.

> **Growing and enjoying native plants serve as subtle reminders of how we need clean water, clean air, and the wildlife that surrounds us, so that we can all live and grow.**

So let's not wait until we're in dire straits before we take action—grow and promote native plants. Let's learn to appreciate native plants as much as we appreciate native fish, deer, bear, wolves, and other critters that make the Great Lakes region such a great place in which to live, work, and play.

With these thoughts in mind, may you go forth and plant natives to your heart's content, knowing that you are doing something positive for yourself and for the environment.

By the way, there is one thing this book is not: it is not a field guide for identifying native wildflowers. See the listing at the end of this book for excellent field guides for identifying wildflowers in the Great Lakes region.

References

Landscaping with Native Plants, Wild Ones, Appleton, WI: 2008.

Tukey, Paul. *Organic Lawn Care Manual: A Natural, Low-Maintenance System for a Beautiful, Safe Lawn*. North Adams, MA: Storey Publishing, LLC, 2007.

3

Taking to the Woods and Fields: Seed Collection

Imagine summer coming to a close here in the Great Lakes region. You can tell because the tourists have deserted some of your favorite places to hike, fish, camp and stroll along looking for wildflowers. The sedges and grasses are starting to look burned out and the flowers on the evening primrose are just past their peak. For most species of wildflowers this is about the time to start collecting seed for later germination.

The first thing to do before collecting seeds from wild plants is get permission from the landowner to harvest the seeds. Fortunately, here in the Great Lakes Region, many folks live in wooded areas, have property up at the cabin or know someone who does, so finding places to harvest seed usually isn't a problem. However, if you don't have an inside on a wild area to collect from, remember that to harvest from state or federal land you will need to visit your local Department of Natural Resources or United States Forest Service headquarters and inquire about a permit or permission to harvest the seed. Another place to look for permission to harvest seed is commercial logging companies, soil conservation districts and nature conservancies.

Okay, you've found a spot to collect seed. Now you'll need to identify the wildflowers. Wildflower identification books (listed in the back of this book)

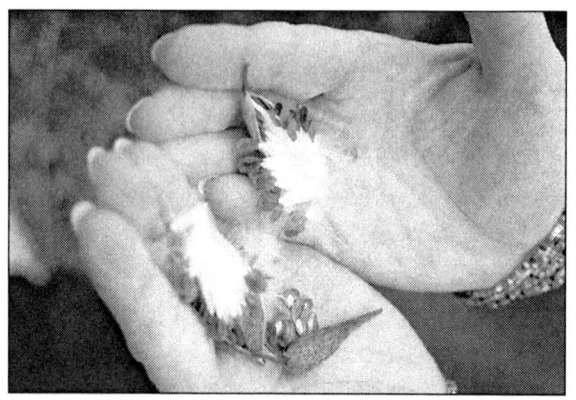 will help you identify the plants you wish to harvest. Find out the best time to go searching for seeds. Most plant identification books give flowering dates for plants, and most plants go to seed shortly after flowering. This will give you a rough idea when to start collecting seeds. Just remember, native plants are about as fickle as the weather they withstand. Wildflowers are a little erratic when it comes to when they'll go to seed each year. The best thing to do is to look for several species of wildflowers when you're foraging—you're sure to find something ready to harvest.

Take a Hike
A few hours spent collecting seed can be as enjoyable as going for a hike. So when you go seed collecting bring along things you would take on a hike, including bug dope, water, and a lunch and some snacks. Also, wear long sleeve shirts and pants and perhaps a floppy hat to protect your face and neck from the sun. Check for ticks before you head home for the day.

You will also need a sharp pair of scissors (actual gardening scissors or "snips" are easier on your fingers and hands than any other type of scissors), some paper bags, and a plant identification book. Another good item to have is a permanent marker to write down what seed is in each bag, and a journal to record the location and date you collected the seed. The tech savvy outdoors person will probably bring a GPS device. A GPS unit will allow you to record exactly where you found some of your prized flora so you can locate it again the following year.

Harvesting the Seed
An understanding of basic plant botany will come in handy in your seed harvesting endeavors. So here goes, botany 101. After the female portion of the flower, called the pistil, has been fertilized by pollen from the anther of the stamen (the

male portion of the flower), seed production begins in the ovary of the pistil. Meanwhile, the flower pedals begin to fade and will eventually fall off. After several days or weeks, seed is produced that will be capable of propagating the species. These seeds are usually green or whitish in appearance initially, then brown or black when mature and ready to harvest.

Some seeds, of course, are surrounded by fruit (which is botanically defined as the covering for the seed). Others are developed in pods, as in legume plants such as a beach pea, and some are in a kind of pouch, such as the seed for coreopsis. And still others are enveloped in a large pod, such as milkweed and has what is commonly referred to as parachutes or fuzzy plant material surrounding the seed. The fuzzy material will aid in the dispersal of the seed.

The domestic plants in our gardens and in our farm fields go to seed in a fairly predictable and uniform manner. Take, for example an ear of corn. All the kernels mature about the same time. If only the same could be said for wildflowers! The ripening of native seed can be erratic within the florescence of the plant, with some seeds ripening one day, the others a few days or weeks later. The ripest seed will generally be found towards the top or terminal ends of the plant. The seeds below may still be green.

A wildflower enthusiast harvesting seed in late summer.

It's critical to harvest the seed when it is ripe; harvest too early and the seed will not be viable, wait too long and the seed may dehisce, which means the seeds eject out of the pod, scattering in the wind or simply falling to the ground. As you can see, seed collecting can be a hit and miss endeavor. However, like a good day of fishing, it is exciting when you hit a lick and come across copious quantities of seeds still intact on the plant.

Distinguishing the seed from other parts of the flower can be challenging for the novice (and experienced) seed collector. What makes it tricky is that seed is often either attached to a "wing," which aids in dispersal of the seed, or a cottony material that in some cases aids in germination of the seed. If you're having trouble distinguishing the seed from the material that surrounds it, do the "kernel test." Place your finger or finger nail over the suspected seed and carefully press down on it. If it feels hard like a kernel of corn, it is most likely the seed.

Seed that is encased within a fruit, such as the red berries of Bunchberry, poses a different challenge. This seed must be removed from the fruit coating and the pulp separated from the seed. The pulp can actually inhibit the germination process. The easiest way to remove the pulp and skins seems to be by mixing the seed with water and putting it through a blender. Or, you can soak it for 48 hours and then remove the pulp by hand the best you can. The seed must then be dried thoroughly on newspaper before it is stored in a paper bag.

There is no one-size-fits all way to harvest the many different plants you will encounter in the wild. Here are some different scenarios that apply to the plants you're apt to encounter in the great outdoors:

For seeds that disperse quickly, such as columbine, cover ripening seed with a sandwich bag and rubber band as soon as the flowers fade to capture the falling seeds.

Some seeds, such as those of pearly everlasting, grow in clusters at the top of a plant within the inflorescence. These can be gently pulled away and will fill a bag in a hurry.

Here is an easy one. On plants such as black-eyed Susan and purple coneflower, clip off the entire seed head and place it in a paper bag. Save the cleaning until you get home.

Berries from native plants are harvested kind of like picking blueberries. However, they can be messy, especially when a little overripe. Place your harvested berries in a plastic re-closable bag or bucket after you pick them and then wait until you get home to separate the pulp. Also, some berries can stain the hands and clothing, so be careful.

Seed Cleaning

Seed cleaning isn't necessary for all seeds, and may even be counter-productive. So who is going to argue with that? In fact, some seeds, such as Canadian wild rye, actually germinate better if they maintain some of the protective material around the seed. When it's necessary or desirable to clean the seed, the simplest way to do it is with various sized screens. Use the screen from a storm door and hardware wire with the smallest squares and any other screens of different sizes you can find. These can be built into simple wooden frames that will last for years. The other, more tedious way is to pick through the chaff. Large seed nurseries use seed cleaning machines for this task.

Seed cleaning isn't necessary for all seeds, and may even be counter-productive.

Yet another method is to use a playing card or similar card and a cafeteria tray or baking tin. Tip the tin or tray so one end is raised and then "rake" the seeds upward on the tin, allowing the seed to roll to the bottom--most of the chaff will stay towards the top of the tray.

Seed cleaning can be a relaxing endeavor or a hair pulling experience, depending on how you approach this task. It will be the former if you get your ducks—and seed cleaning equipment—in a row before you start. Here is what you need to get started:

1. Seed cleaning screens or sifters;
2. Fast food serving tray, baking tin or similar flat surface with sides;
3. One playing card (no, we're not playing poker!);
4. Magnifying glass (optional);
5. Water proof storage container;
6. Comfortable chair;
7. Your favorite music and beverage.

Okay, you've got the seed home and cleaned. The next thing is storage. Again, there are a lot of

Members of the Northern Wild Plant & Seed Cooperative demonstrate seed cleaning.

variables involved in storing native seeds, especially in keeping it viable until it is time to plant. Immediately after the seed is harvested it should be allowed to dry in the open air for a couple of days, preferably by spreading it out on newspaper. This can be done anywhere where there is good air flow, including a greenhouse. Once dried, it can be stored in clear plastic bins in an unheated building, refrigerator or even a freezer. Follow these tips for successful seed storage:

1. Store in plastic bins that won't absorb moisture;
2. Avoid excessive heat, dryness or humidity;
3. Store in a dark place;
4. Check periodically for signs of rodents;
5. Do not store in plastic sandwich bags.

> When you go seed collecting bring along things you would take on a hike, including bug dope, water and a lunch or some snacks. Also, wear a long sleeve shirt and pants and perhaps a floppy hat to protect your face and neck from the sun. Check for ticks before you head home for the day.

References

Protocol Information. Hiawatha National Forest Native Plant Program, USFS.

Riley, Edward H. and Carroll L. Shry Jr. *Introductory Horticulture.* 6th ed. Albony, NY: Delmar-Thomson Learning, 2002.

4

Seed Germination Secrets Revealed

Growing native plants from seed is kind of like predicting the weather around the Great Lakes. Sometimes you get it right, and sometimes, well, you're a little off. The fun, of course, is in the challenge.

The plants chosen in this book represent the ones I and others in the business have experience in planting. The directions and tips on propagation were gleaned from a variety of rather limited sources, as footnoted, but mostly from my own experience growing native wildflowers. It is by no means the final say on how to germinate each species. If there is one thing I've found out in the past few years of experimenting with native seeds, it is that just when you think there is only one way to germinate a certain species, you discover another way to do it, or at least, an exception to the rule.

These plants were grown in a state-of-the-art greenhouse by the Otsego Soil Conservation District.

For instance, for many years I believed the only way to germinate mountain ash (*Sorbus* species) seed was by soaking them in an acid solution that would mimic the natural stratification or scarification that supposedly takes place in the digestive tract of an animal. Then one day I witnessed how some *Sorbus* seed, left in a moist medium in a refrigerator for a few weeks, had germinated…in the dark, and in the cold! So go figure.

The point is to experiment. Nature is unpredictable and there are many variables that effect seed germination, such as when it was harvested, how it was stored, its overall viability, and even how it is handled (for instance, the membranes of native seeds can actually be damaged in the process of cleaning and sorting the seed).

Sound daunting? Not really, but it is challenging. If your initial attempt fails to germinate a particular species, try another approach. For example, if after a one-month cold, moist stratification period you only achieve 20% germination, try a one-month cold, followed by one-month warm, stratification. See if it germinates better with the latter approach. You'll be tickled pink when you learn nature's script and figure out how to germinate a specific species of wildflower. Bear in mind, though, that for some seed, if you get 50% or better germination, you're doing fine (compared to up to 95% with commercial seed).

> Use a journal to record all the details of this project, including how and when it was stratified and details regarding germination (such as when it was brought into the heat, how the seed was covered, etc.).

Native vs. Primed Seed

Native seeds are quite different from the ones we buy from seed companies, such as Burpee and Jung. Catalog varieties, such as the Hybrid Northern X-tra Sweet Corn I grow in my vegetable garden, have been crossbred a number of times to improve on many traits, including seed vigor. Also, commercial seeds are primed, which means they've been given a chemical or water treatment that ensures success if planted in favorable conditions.

On the other hand, native seeds have a scripted plan for germination, which is only shared by mother nature. Most native plants have evolved to germinate only under certain conditions, and they may require some type of stratification to germinate, such as a month of cold, moist conditions. Some native plants even need to be scarified, or have the seed coat nicked, to aid in what is called radical emergence. The challenge, of course, is to find out the seed germination requirements for the seeds of a particular native plant and replicate it the best you can in a greenhouse, refrigerator, or outside in a garden bed.

It is imperative, when experimenting with native plants, to keep a journal to log your successes and failures. Record things like date started, methods used to stratify or scarify the seeds, planting depth, time it took to germinate, percentage of germination, when it was transplanted, and any other information that may help you next time around.

Starting Seed in a Greenhouse or Cold Frame
There are basically two ways to germinate native seed. One way is to simply sow the seed in a permanent spot outdoors. This is best done in the fall. The seed is simply sown or broadcast into loose soil that has been worked up with a rototiller or farm implements. This seed will undergo a natural stratification process and will most likely germinate in the spring.

If you're looking to grow transplants that can be sold or transported to a specific site, you will need to start them inside in flats or pots. This process starts with the proper selection of a germination medium. The best medium for germination and "growing on" is a sterile, non-soil medium containing sphagnum peat moss, vermiculite, and perlite. These come pre-mixed and go by the trade names Sunshine, Bacto, and Premier Pro-mix. Much of this stuff comes via Canada and works well for most situations which call for a sterile mix that absorbs water well but also drains well.

These mixes can be purchased most economically in a

Seeds should be started in a shallow container with good drainage.

compressed 3.8 cu. ft. bag from nurseries, or special-ordered from a feed store or nursery supply catalog. Mixes also come in smaller bags of loose mix. Other useful things to have on hand are filtered sand and vermiculite, which are sometimes used for seeds which must be sown under special conditions, such as close to the surface. In this case, vermiculite is sprinkled sparingly over the exposed seed to aid in germination.

Seed started in a greenhouse or grow house will require a stratification period prior to germination, which is explained below. Since the natives in this book are perennial, just like hosta and delphinium, they should be sown in January or February in a heated greenhouse. This means a stratification period would have to begin up to two months (depending on the species) prior to actually being sown in a greenhouse or grow house.

Seed Treatment Methods
Contained within the description for each of the native flowers featured in this book are propagation instructions for each species. Let's take a look at what these processes entail.

Stratification
After seed is formed in the late summer and fall, it is, in most cases, scattered about and then lies dormant over the long, cold winter. This is a natural stratification process that obviously occurs with no help from us. This process not only softens the seed coat for germination, but also helps to trigger the seed into germinating when the conditions are right. We can mimic these conditions by doing our own stratification. After years of trial and error, where as I tried various methods to stratify seeds (including cold out buildings and snow banks), I've found the best way to stratify native seed is in a refrigerator, where the temperature and humidity is consistent.

> **After much experimentation and some failures, the best way I've found to provide a cold stratification period for seeds is to place them in a refrigerator.**

Moist stratification is the most common technique employed to encourage germination of native seed. Employ this technique by simply placing the seed in a moist (not wet—the medium should never be dripping) medium. This medium could consist of simple potting mix containing peat moss, vermiculite, and perlite. Some folks have also reported success using oak or pine sawdust since it is easy to work with and will wick moisture into the seed itself. The high acid content reportedly keeps bacteria in check.

Note: when mixing water with a growing medium for stratifying seeds (or germinating seed for that matter), add one part water to three parts medium. This should give you a moist, but not dripping wet, medium to work with.

The easiest method of stratification is a simple cold stratification with no growing medium. This is called dry stratification. You simply place the seed in a refrigerator or freezer (depending on what the seed calls for) and then sow it after it has stratified for the recommended period of time. These times can vary from two weeks to over thirty days. Keep the seed from taking on too much dampness by placing the dried seeds in a plastic sealed container. This method works particularly well for some easy-to-grow types, such as Canada wild rye.

A cold, moist stratification period involves mixing the seed into a moist medium as explained above. You don't need much medium to do the job. I've used chewing tobacco tins, filled to the top with a few hundred seeds mixed into the medium. Place the tin in the refrigerator for the recommended period of time.

Some collected seed may require a cold-moist stratification period followed by a warm-moist stratification period. This involves simply providing a cold, moist stratification period as mentioned above, and then transferring the seed and medium to a warmer environment, such as a warm greenhouse or room, for the recommended time period. This method is recommended for hard-to-germinate species, such as Joe-pye weed, and species that won't germinate any other way.

If you are ever in doubt about what stratification method to use, harvest the seed when it first ripens and direct seed in the ground, much like mother nature intended.

Scarification

Seeds shifting in the coarse grains of sand or spilling over rocks in a stream brings to mind the natural process of scarification. We can easily replicate this action by nicking the seed coat with an emery board or fine sand paper. This method is required of some plants that have tough coated seeds, such as iris and baptisia. Be sure to check if a period of moist stratification is needed after the seed is scarified.

Well, there it is. I just told you all I know about getting native seeds to sprout. Go ahead, give it a try and let me know how you make out.

References

Powell, Eileen, *Seed to Bloom: How to Grow over 500 Annuals, Perennials & Herbs*, North Adams, MA: Storey Books, 1995.

5

Starting Selected Wildflowers from Seed

Over the past twelve years I've been involved in propagating various native plants that are found in the forests and along the shoreline of the Great Lakes region. These plants were used for plant restoration projects by nonprofit groups as well as in home gardens. I've talked with groups and individuals who share my interest in native plants. From these conversations and experiences I've been able to narrow down what I believe to be the most popular and, with a few exceptions, easiest wildflowers to propagate.

The below list of plants is by no means an exhaustive list of the native plants found in the region. I've presented these selected plants in this chapter to give you the information you'll need to successfully germinate and establish them in a flower bed, meadow, etc. I'm sure I've missed someone's favorite wildflower or even a type that is easy to propagate and should be mentioned.

It should also be said that propagating wildflowers is not an exact science. The propagation information presented below is simply what has worked for myself and others. Experimentation is the rule when propagating wildflowers. If a particular method of stratification isn't working-- for instance, a cold, moist stratification period-- try a cold, moist stratification period followed by a warm, moist stratification period.

North Country Gardening with Wildflowers

Over the years myself and fellow members of the Northern Plant and Seed Cooperative have identified certain species of wildflowers that are easy to grow and maintain. We call these plants work horses, because they'll work hard at establishing themselves wherever they're planted. If you're just starting to grow wildflowers, we suggest you include these reliable native plants in your flower beds and other places you desire native wildflowers.

> Lanceleaf Coreopsis (*Coreopsis lancelolata L.*)
> Black-eyed Susan (*Rudbeckia hirta L.*)
> Evening Primrose (*Oenothera biennis*)
> Asters (*Aster sp.*)
> Goldenrod (*Salidago Canadensis*)
> Bee Balm (*Monarda fistulosa L.*)

I hope you'll rise to the challenge and attempt to grow some of these wildflower favorites-- for the good of the critters and perhaps the planet. But most of all, have fun growing native wildflowers and learn more about your natural heritage so you can pass it down to your children and grandchildren.

 Agrimony

Agrimony is a "sturdy" wildflower that will hold its own once established. The seeds of this native wildflower can stick to your clothing when you brush up against it. This could be a good thing as you could be spreading it to a new locale.

The long stems of agrimony bear small yellow flowers. Ht. to 5'.

Where it grows: Agrimony is found in the woods and along the weedy perimeters of old hay fields. It will grow in fairly damp, clay soils. Hardy to zone 4.

Seed collection: The bur which contains the seed is rather conspicuous at the end of a spiked stalk. Collect the seed in late summer to fall.

Propagation: Mainly by seed after soaking for 24 hours, then providing a three-week cold stratification period.

Planting depth: ¼"

Agrimonia gryposepala

Bee Balm, aka Wild Bergamot

Bee balm is to butterflies and hummingbirds what sunflowers are to songbirds. Plant bee balm and you're virtually guaranteed to attract these critters, which flock to the pinkish-red flowers. This is an easy-to-grow native plant that can be divided in 2–3 years. Bee balm is a member of the mint family so it's no wonder the foliage gives off a fragrant scent when crushed. Native Americans made Oswego Tea of the leaves. Contemporary teas are made from bergamot leaves.

Lavender-pink flowers bloom from mid-summer to early fall. Ht. 2–4'.

Where to plant: Prefers well-drained soil and is often found in open prairies, pine woodalands, fields, rocky or gravelly sites and roadsides. Hardy to zone 4.

Seed collection: Bee balm produces nut-like seeds measuring about 1/16" in diameter. It is typically harvested in October. Cut the seed head then shake out the seed. You can garner more seeds by rubbing the seed heads by hand. The seeds are small and black. It isn't necessary to clean the chaff from the seed.

Propagation: Simply dry the seeds in an open paper bag or plastic container, then store in a cool, dry place until ready to plant. No need to provide a moist stratification for this one.

Planting depth: Just cover.

Monarda fistulosa L.

5: Starting Selected Wildflowers from Seed

Bellwort, Large-Flowered

Bellwort was once thought to be able to cure diseases of the throat due simply to the fact that its flowers hang down much like the uvula in your throat. Native Americans mixed bellwort and boneset to create an infusion to relieve sore backs and other muscle ailments. Its flowers hang forlornly from the central stem. Spring flowering bellwort is a good choice for those upland areas of beech-maple hardwoods and hemlock. It is also at home in low flood plain woods and streamside thickets.

Yellow flowers bloom in April and May. Ht. to about 18".

Where it plant: Bellwort will grow in both upland and lowland areas. Prefers shade to partial shade; it's a good choice for a woodland garden. Zones 3–8.

Seed collection: The seed is a triangular fruit and is harvested in June. The seed of Bellwort need not be cleaned.

Propagation: Seed immediately after harvesting, if possible. If not, provide a cold, moist stratification period of one month prior to attempting to germinate it in a greenhouse, or under propagation light indoors.

Planting depth: Just cover.

Uvularia grandiflora

Big blue stem

You may know this mainstay of the prairie as "turkey foot." Big blue stem is a hardy grass for the northern areas and an excellent source of food for wildlife. There is something about this grass of the prairies that will make you want to include it in your flower bed, prairie or meadow planting. Perhaps it is how it compliments flowering native plants or how the stems turn a deep burgundy color in the fall.

Burgundy foliage from this clumping plant is impressive waying in the breeze. Ht. to 5'.

Where to plant: Big blue stem occurs along roadsides, existing and old railroad grades, jack pine plains and oak savannas. It does best in sandy, well-drained soil and tolerates clay. Hardy to zone 4.

Seed collection: The seed is an achene and is collected as the fall colors peak. The seed is stripped from the stalk but doesn't require cleaning.

Propagation: Dry the seeds for 1-2 weeks in open paper bags. Keep in a cool, dry place until planted. It can be stored for up to three years. Sow the seed on top of the soil. Big blue stem can be easily divided after two to three years.

Planting depth: Cover lightly

Andropogon gerardii vitman

5: Starting Selected Wildflowers from Seed

Black-eyed Susan

Black-eyed Susan is an easy-to-grow, short-lived perennial. A grouping of these bright yellow flowers with the "black eye" is quite a site indeed. This is a good one to plant if you want early success with native plants. They're found throughout the United States and are actually native to the Western U.S. It is a host plant for beneficial insects and a good nectar source for bees.

Yellow flowers are prevalent throughout the summer months and into fall. Ht. 1–3'.

Where to plant: The nice thing about this plant is it can tolerate many different soil types—even stubborn clay! Grow in full sun or partial shade, savannas, barrens, open areas and meadows. Hardy to zone 4.

Seed collection: Seed is easy to collect. Simply clip the seed heads while you're in the field and shake out the seeds when you get back home over a cup or glass of your favorite beverage. These black pebble-like seeds can be collected from August to October.

Propagation: Seed and division. Black-eyed Susan seed doesn't need any special treatment and can be sown in containers in late winter in a greenhouse or direct seeded in the spring or fall in cultivated soil. If you have difficulty with germination, a cold, moist stratification of 2–4 weeks should be sufficient.

Planting depth: Surface sow.

Rudbeckia hirta L.

Bloodroot

This plant gets its name from the bright red sap that is revealed when it is injured. Native Americans used the sap as a dye for making clothing. The dye was also used for ceremonial body painting. Bloodroot is poisonous, so it is limited medicinally.

White flowers bloom in the spring. Ht. from 2–6".

Where to plant: Bloodroot is found in rich soil under the tree canopy in forested areas. Mix a generous amount of compost into your soil before planting in a partially shaded area. Zones 3–9.

Seed collection: Bloodroot seed is easy to collect. Look for a capsule which starts to form by early summer, soon after the petals fall off. The leaves will continue to grow, sometimes concealing the seed. The seed is ripe when swollen and yellow to brown in color.

Propagation: Although bloodroot is a rhizome, research seems to confirm that it is best propagated by seed. The seed is most viable if planted immediately after harvest. If that's not possible, store it in a moist medium and plant as soon as possible.

Planting depth: Cover lightly.

Sanguinaria canadensis

Blue Cohosh

Blue Cohosh was used medicinally by Native Americans for problems surrounding childbirth and pregnancy. It is a fascinating plant to look at and provides interest throughout the season. The emerging leaves are a violet-gray color as they eventually unfold to look like a giant columbine (also making it easy to identify). You'll get a kick out of the deep blue berries that form in late summer.

Lavender-purple flowers bloom in late spring. Ht. From 1–3'.

Where to plant: Cohosh is associated with limestone soils, though it will grow well in other locales, providing the soil is rich in organic matter and stays moist throughout the season. Applying lime to the soil will improve plant vigor and color. Hardy to zone 4.

Seed collection: The seed, which looks like a berry, is collected in late summer, about the time the mosquito population starts to dwindle. Don't worry about storing the seed as it needs to be planted right away.

Propagation: Although the seed of blue cohosh appears as a fruit, it is really a seed with a hard outer seed coat. Scarify the seed coat soon after harvest by placing it in a blender with water and flipping the switch. Alternatively, you can soak the seed at least 24 hours. The scarified seed should be sown immediately outdoors in open soil or a cold frame. If starting this one in a greenhouse, be patient; it can take up to two years to germinate!

Caulophyllum thalictroides

Planting depth: Just cover

Blue Flag Iris

It seems most flower gardens sport a nice clump of iris. Fortunately, there is a native type that fits the bill for wildflower lovers in the Great Lakes region. The native species is just as beautiful as any fancy hybrid, in my opinion. Native Americans had a use for blue flag iris: they turned the flowers into a paste and used it to treat liver ailments.

As the name denotes, the blooms are blue. It flowers in early summer. Ht. to 2'.

Where to Plant: Prefers standing water or saturated muck for most of the season. This can be found in a border of a swampy or wetland area on your property at home or at the cabin. You could also plant blue flag iris in a submersible pot and place it in the shallow area of a water garden. Zones 4–9.

Seed collection: The pods of blue flag iris are large and conspicuous. Harvest in mid-summer after it ripens.

Propagation: Like any iris, it has a rhizome that makes it easy to propagate from division. The seed should be cold-moist stratified for one month before planting. It will take 2–3 years to flower if sown from seed.

Planting depth: Surface sow

Iris versicolor L.

BONESET

Boneset is a great choice to include in a rain garden or marshy area. It's also kind of a tough guy; once established it will hold its own for many years. It has a dense set of white flowers borne on the top of the plant in flat clusters. It attracts several species of butterflies, including the yellow swallowtail, great spangled fritillary and painted lady.

White flowers bloom in summer and early fall. Ht. 18" to 5'.

Where to plant: Will grow best in marshy areas and wet ditches. Instead of filling in low spots with fill soil, plant a rain garden and include boneset and other marsh plants. These plants will effectively filter rain water, helping to replenish aquifers and ultimately attract frogs, dragon flies and the like. Tolerates partial shade. Zones 3–9.

Seed collection: The seed can be harvested in the fall. Watch for the seed heads to dry and split. There is no need to separate the seed from the fuzzy material.

Propagation: Seed and tip cuttings. Seeds of boneset can be a bugger to germinate. Like many difficult-to-germinate natives, if they fail to germinate in the greenhouse, I direct seed them in the fall in a cultivated sandy-loam soil. Another method is to soak the seed in sulfuric acid for 24 hours and then provide three month warm, followed by three month cold treatment. Experimentation is the rule with this one.

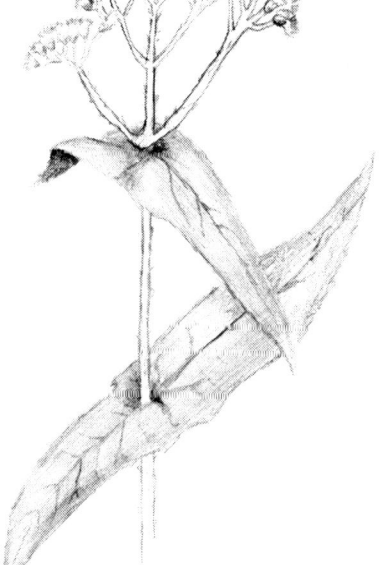

Eupatorium perfoliatum

Planting depth: Just cover

Bunchberry

It's hard to believe that bunchberry is in the same genus as flowering dogwood. It is much shorter in stature than the other *Cornus* species, but not in beauty. It forms a ground cover in the understory of the forest and spreads by underground rhizomes. Bunchberry is truly a harbinger of spring. Look for the white flower petals (actually called bracts) first thing after the weather has warmed and after a nice rain. Deer and other animals of the north woods take a liking to the berries.

White flowers of bunchberry usher in spring in the woodland forest. Ht. 8–10".

Where to plant: Bunchberry prefers the shady understory of trees or tall shrubbery and an acid soil. A neutral soil can be made more acidic by adding sulfur. Zones 2–6.

Seed collection: Collect the berries of bunchberry in late summer.

Propagation: Bunchberry can be propagated by division. The other way to propagate bunchberry is to remove the seed from the berries and provide a one month cold, moist stratification period, or leave in a cold frame throughout the winter and then plant in a greenhouse or outdoors in the spring. Yet another way to propagate it is by the buds that form along the withered stem or along the roots in the fall of the year. Simply spread these out along the soil in the spring and cover with soil.

Cornus Canadensis

Planting depth: ¼"

Butterfly Weed

Butterfly weed (aka butterfly milkweed) looks like anything but a weed. The cluster of bright orange flowers at the top of this sturdy plant is very appealing to the eye. A steady supply of nectar through most of the summer serves as an attractant for butterflies and beneficial bees. Butterfly weed is in the same genus as milkweed.

This plant, with its orange clusters on top of branching stems, Blooms for the better part of the summer. Ht. 1–2'.

Where to plant: Butterfly weed prefers full sun and will tolerate some tough soils, though they seem to grow best in sand or in even gravelly soil. It is a plant that will colonize, so space them at least a foot apart and allow them to fill in the spaces. This plant is showy enough to include in a flower bed along the foundation of a home, or in rock gardens. Zones 3–9.

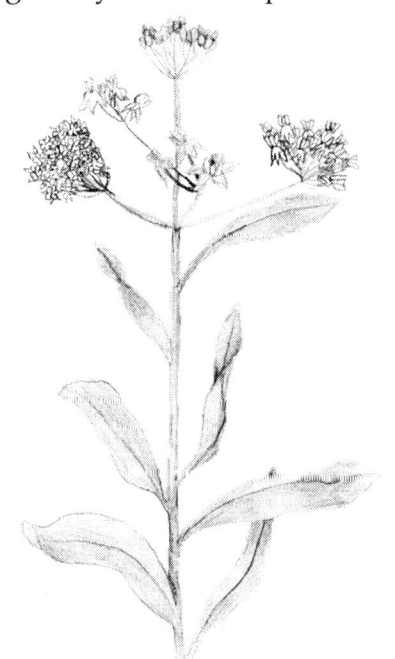

Seed collection: Butterfly weed produces an abundance of seed. Pick when seeds have turned brown.

Propagation: Although easy to propagate, the milkweeds don't lend themselves well to being cramped up in flats or pots in a greenhouse. Grow in peat pots or plant as quickly as possible after they've established themselves well in the greenhouse. The other alternative of course, is to direct seed in the fall outdoors.

Planting depth: Just cover.

Asclepias tuberosa

Canada Anemone

A good time to plant warm season vegetables (corn, squash, etc.) in the north is when you see the anemone blooming in the fields. The rather large, white pedals of the anemone are hard to miss massed together along the weedy borders of open hayfields, which are a common site where I live here in the Eastern Upper Peninsula of Michigan.

White pedals bloom for a brief period in early summer. Grows from 1–2'.

Where to plant: Plant Canada anemone where it can naturally spread by rhizomes. It appears to prefer sandy-loam to slightly clay soil. Zones 3–9.

Seed collection: Harvest the seeds of Canada anemone in mid to late summer, immediately after the cottony seed heads have started to disintegrate.

Propagation: The seed will germinate best if sown right after harvest, although I've had good results after storing them for a year and then provide one month of cool, moist stratification.

Planting depth: Just cover.

Anemone canadensis

Canada Wild Rye

Canada wild rye is a good choice to plant as a part of a dune restoration project along the Great Lakes shoreline, its preferred habitat. It is a good choice as a plant to slow erosion or to simply fill in an area with a food source for wildlife. Grown in a clump, Canada wild rye is impressive swaying in the breeze.

Heavy plumes of white flowers nod and sway in the breeze. Ht. 4–5'.

Where to plant: Grows well in most soils, including clay. Canada wild rye will grow tallest in a sunny location. Hardy to zone 4.

Seed collection: The seed is normally harvested from September to October. Look for the seed to turn yellow when ripened. It is easily harvested by stripping the seeds off the stalk. The seed need not be cleaned; that is, the chafe and husk need not be removed from the seed itself. Dried seed will stay viable for up to three years when stored in a cool, dry place.

Propagation: This seed can be dried in a paper bag or rubberized container for the 1–2 week drying period required before planting. Moist stratification is unnecessary. Surface sow Canada wild rye by pressing the seed gently into the growing medium.

Planting depth: Cover lightly.

Elymus canadensis

Clintonia

Clintonia is another of the spring collection of plants growing in a woodland setting. With its petite yellow flowers, clintonia doesn't exactly shout out at you as you hike through the forest, but it is impressive all the same. Look for clintonia, aka bluebead lily, among bunchberry and wintergreen in partially shaded areas.

This spring flowering wildflower has yellow mostly nodding flowers. Ht. 6–15".

Where to plant: Plant clintonia among the woodland plants. Its short stature makes it a good candidate for a rock garden. Zones 2–6.

Seed collection: Clintonia produces a (toxic) deep blue berry from August to September. Separate the seed from the pulp (use protective gloves for this task) and let it soak in water for at least 24 hours. Finish cleaning as best you can, then let dry on newspaper and store in a plastic container or paper bag in a cool, dry place until time to plant.

Propagation: Difficult to start from seed. Alternating moist, cold, and moist, warm stratification periods for one month each will help coax it to germinate. Clintonia is much easier to propagate from division, though it shouldn't be plucked from the wild for this purpose.

Planting depth: Just cover.

Clintonia borealis

Columbine

Columbine is a great harbinger of spring. Native Americans used columbine to remedy certain maladies, as a love potion, and even as a cologne for men. They also smoked the seeds for good luck. It is pollinated by hummingbirds and some moths, so expect to see these critters when it is flowering.

Reddish flowers with yellow centers. Blooms in late spring. Ht. To 3'.

Where to plant: Look for columbine in shady, sandy, and sandy loam soils. Zones 3–9.

Seed collection: Collect seed in early summer. Gather the seeds soon after flowering, otherwise they will drop from the pods and be eaten by the birds, which isn't necessarily a bad thing, now is it? Seeds are small, black, pebble like and are easy to harvest, clean and store.

Propagation: Cold stratify for up to four weeks in a cold, moist medium in a refrigerator. Columbine can be planted in flats or small trays in a greenhouse. It also can be direct seeded in early spring or fall.

Planting depth: Surface sow.

Aquilegia canadensis

Coneflower, Cut-leaved

Cut-leaved coneflower is a marvelously conspicuous plant. It grows 4-8 feet and has bright yellow flowers. It flowers during the peak period of summer into September. The showy coneflower prefers mostly sunny locations. It can be used to naturalize a woodland area, as cut flowers, or in a cottage garden.

Bright yellow flowers bloom all summer and into the fall. Ht. 3–10'.

Where to plant: Will grow in wet, swampy areas and clay soils. Zones 3–9.

Seed collection: Seed is collected during the chilly months of October and November. The seed is small, round, black and is easy to harvest.

Propagation: Coneflower seed responds well to a cold stratification period of one to three months. It can be cold stored up to three years.

Planting depth: Surface sow.

Rudbeckia laciniata

Evening Primrose

The dog days of summer are fast approaching when you see the beautiful bright yellow blossoms of evening primrose. It got the name, primrose because of its scent, which reminded people of the old world primroses, though it is native to North America. It is a biennial that is a favorite of the goldfinches; the birds will feed from the seed pods all year long. Evening primrose attracts various butterflies, including fritillaries and monarchs, not to mention pollinating bees.

Yellow flowers bloom for a fairly short period in August. Ht. 2–5'.

Where to plant: I associate evening primrose mostly with roadsides, but they also show up in fields alongside Queen Anne's lace and common mullein. This plant is adaptable to most soil types. Evening primrose can overwhelm a small garden bed, so plant where it has room to spread or be contained, whichever is desired. Zones 4–9.

Seed collection: Seeds form in capsules or pods and mature and turn brown in late summer into fall. Allow the pods to dry then shake the tiny seeds out onto a paper plate. Separate the chafe from the seed the best you can.

Propagation: Evening primrose propagates easily from seed. A cold, moist stratification period will ensure good germination. It is easy to divide as well.

Planting depth: Surface sow.

Oenothera biennis

False Solomon's Seal

Another fine specimen of the woodland garden, false Soloman's seal is sure to please. It will fill in empty spaces as the rhizomes spread horizontally beneath the surface of the soil. You'll marvel at the grape-like clusters of mostly purple berries produced in the fall.

Flowers in spring to early summer. Ht. 16" to 3'.

Where to plant: Prefers a moist wetland habitat, though I've seen it in drier soils. False Solomon's seal will grow best in a partially shaded area in mostly sandy soil. Zones 3–8.

Seed collection: Berries turn white initially then spotted with purple in the autumn. Separate seed from the pulp. An overnight soaking or trip through a blender with water will help clean it sufficiently for eventual storage.

Propagation: Sow outside immediately after cleaning. Otherwise, propagate by dividing rhizomes in the fall.

Planting depth: Just cover

Smilacina racemosa

Fringed Brome

Grasses certainly don't draw the attention to themselves from humans as do wildflowers--but that's okay, the animals love them! Grasses like fringed brome are an important cog in the local ecology. In addition, they look quite elegant swaying in the breeze on a warm summer day.

Fringed brome adds visual interest and texture to a garden. Ht. 1–2'.

Where to plant: Fringed brome is found in thickets, stream banks, moist shores, openings in cedar bogs, ditches and other wet places. It grows in clumps up to two feet high. Plant accordingly. Hardy to zone 4.

Seed collection: Seed is an achene and is harvested from July to September. It need not be cleaned prior to storing or planting.

Propagation: Provide a cold, moist stratification of at least one month. It can be cold stored for up to three years. Direct seed outside in the spring or fall or start inside in a greenhouse or cold frame. If starting fringe brome inside a greenhouse, don't leave them in the flats very long as their roots don't like to be crowded in the tiny cell packs.

Planting depth: Just cover.

Bromus ciliatus L.

Gentian, Bottled

Bottled or closed gentian has a long and noble history. It was named after Gentius, King of Illyrian (who ruled 181-168 B.C.). Historians believe he had discovered that the herb can be used as a tonic. The tonic is made from the bitter root of the plant.

Blue, violet or white, egg-shaped flowers bloom in late summer-fall. Ht. 18"to 3'.

Where to plant: Bottled or closed gentian likes moist conditions. Use for a meadow or woodland planting where it is moist and partly sunny. Zones 3–9.

Seed collection: Copious quantities of seed can be collected in the fall. You will know the seed is ripe when it begins to split.

Propagation: This strikingly beautiful plant is worth the difficulties you may encounter propagating it. The best method of seed germination may be to surface sow outside and cover lightly with coarse sand.

Planting depth: Surface sow.

Gentiana andrewsii

Goldenrod, Canada

If goldenrod were dollars I'd be a rich man! This one grows prolifically in the field next to my garden. Hence, I need to shake off the notion it is just a weed. To the contrary, it is a very useful plant in the natural landscape. I've observed the flowers peppered with pollinating bumble bees. Also, the seeds of goldenrod provide food for wildlife in winter and a home for insects (inside round "galls" on the stems).

Golden-yellow flowers bloom from mid-summer into fall. Grows to 2'.

Where to plant: Another nice thing about this wild plant is it is adaptable for most sites, including clay, sand, and loam. Zones 2–8.

Seed collection: Gather copious quantities of seed in late fall to early winter.

Propagation: Cold stratify for one month in a moist medium, then start in a greenhouse or grow house, or direct seed in fall.

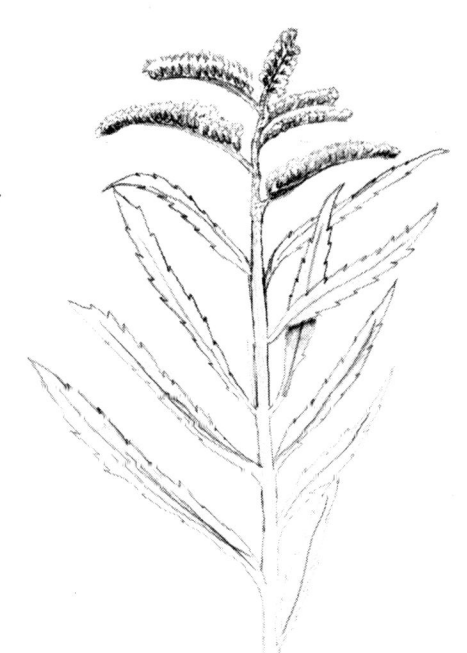

Planting depth: Just cover

Salidago canadensis

Harebell (Bluebells)

Harebell, sometimes called bluebells was, or perhaps still is used by Native Americans for the treatment of coughs and tuberculosis.

Blue-violet bell-shaped-flowers bloom starting in spring and well into the summer. Ht. 12–18".

Where to plant: Grows in rocky outcrops, dry woodlands and sandy shorelines. It prefers full sun to light shade. Its adoring bloom persists from June to September. Zones 3–9.

Seed collection: The tiny seed is harvested in late September.

Propagation: Like many native plants, the seed of harebell need not be cleaned. That is, the fussy material attached to the seed need not be separated from the seed. It requires a moist stratification of one to three months and will store up to three years in cold, mostly dry conditions.

Planting depth: Surface sow

Campanula rotundifolia

Hepatica, Round Lobed

Hepatica is another harbinger of spring. It could be dubbed the "African violet of the north," due to its resemblance to this common houseplant.

The violet flowers bloom in early spring. Ht. 3–6".

Where to plant: Prefers partial shade with good air movement. Soil should be rich in humus (that is, compost in an advanced state of decay). It is an ideal plant for a woodland setting and rock gardens. Planting in drifts will keep them from becoming over powered by other wildflowers. Zones 3–8.

Seed collection: While most seeds turn brown or black when ripe, hepatica is the exception. The seeds turn green when ripe and the only way of knowing they're ready to be harvested is in the ease in which they are released from the stem. Look for ripe seeds about four weeks after they bloom.

Propagation: Sow outdoors immediately after collection, if possible. If you're not able to plant right away, store in a moist medium in the refrigerator.

Planting depth: ¼".

Hepatica americana

Jack-in-the-Pulpit

Here is a peculiar plant that conceals its flower in a cup-shaped spathe. It's a plant that really makes you pause to have a closer look when you're hiking in the woods. I've observed Jack-in-a-pulpit in a lowland area of young deciduous trees and shrubs near my home. It flowers in the early spring and produces red (poisonous) berries.

Lavender-purple flowers bloom in spring. Ht. 8"–24".

Where to plant: Plant in shady areas among mostly deciduous trees and shrubs. Zones 3–9.

Seed collection: The berries may be hard to come by due to the feeding habits of wildlife and the limited quantities of fruit on each plant. Start looking for the ripe berries in the fall, but be careful when cleaning the pulp away from the seed as it can be a skin irritant for some folks.

Propagation: Propagating Jack-in-the-pulpit by seed can be a little difficult, but it is possible. It needs a 90-day cold period at 40 degrees, followed by germination at 70 degrees. Separating the corms is easy though, which can be done in the fall after the plant dies off.

Planting depth: Surface sow

Arisaema triphyllum

5: Starting Selected Wildflowers from Seed

Jewelweed (Touch-me-not)

Jewelweed is aptly named because the leaves of the plant repel water, forming little droplets of water on the leaves. The droplets look like little jewels, especially as the morning sun streams through the lowland areas where it grows. It is also called touch-me-not and snapweed, because when touched, the dried seed pods actually fling the seed hither and yon, so keep this in mind when harvesting the seed. Jewelweed self seeds abundantly.

Yellow-orange flowers bloom from summer to early fall. Ht. 2–5'.

Where to plant: Plant jewelweed in wetland areas and abandoned ditches. Instead of draining beneficial wetland areas on your property, why not plant jewelweed and other plants that like it wet? Hardy to zone 4.

Seed collection: As mentioned above, the capsules explode (they dehisce, in botany parlance) out of the pods, so you'll have fun gathering the seeds for this one. This is a job best suited for the quick hands of a youngster! It is harvested in late August through October.

Propagation: The seed need not be cleaned. Cold stratify for at least two months before planting.

Planting depth: Surface sow

Impatiens capensis

Joe-Pye Weed

Joe-pye weed is an excellent plant to use to add some vertical appeal to a low lying wetland or marshy area, including clay sites. I'm using it to fill in a low ditch next to my driveway. It's one less place I have to mow! Just make sure to plant it in a fairly sunny spot. It grows to five feet and has rather striking light purple flowers in clusters at the top of the plant. It blooms from July to September.

Pinkish-lavender flowers bloom from summer to early fall. Ht. 2–6'.

Where to plant: Joe-pye weed is found mostly in low-lying areas near creek beds and in ditches, so plant accordingly. Hardy to zone 4.

Seed collection: The seed is an achene and is harvested in October. Save time by cutting the terminal or top portion of the plant and separating the seed when you get back home. The seed need not be cleaned.

Propagation: Experimentation is in order with this one. Germination success varies. Provide a cool, moist stratification for at least two months in a refrigerator. You may have better luck by direct seeding in a moist, sandy bed outdoors in the fall. It transplants fairly easily from cell packs or a seed bed.

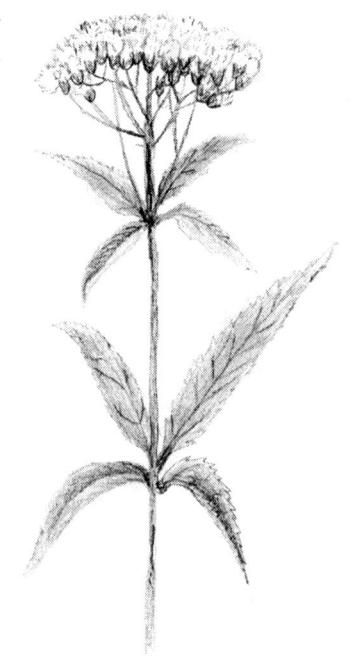

Planting depth: Just cover

Eupatorium maculatum

Lanceleaf Coreopsis

This wildflower with the bright as sunshine yellow flowers has been dubbed by our native plant and seed co-op as one of the "work horses" of the wildflower world. It gets this distinction because it is easy to grow from seed, adapts well to most soils and really stands out. Song birds will appreciate the seed source. And that's not all, the painted ladies and buckeye butterflies will use this plant as a source for nectar.

Bright yellow flowers bloom during the summer months. Ht. 2–3'.

Where to plant: Coreopsis favors full sun to partial shade. It will grow in most soil types and conditions including sandy shorelines, alvars (shallow soil over limestone rock) and even rocky soils. Zones 3–9.

Seed collection: You can procrastinate a bit before you go to the field to gather seeds of coreopsis because it holds them in a pod for quite some time. They're ripe and ready to pick in late August and into September. The seed heads can be picked and taken home to be cleaned.

Propagation: Easily propagates by seed and division. Let the seed dry one to two weeks in open paper bags or plastic containers. Shake occasionally to aid in drying. Native coreopsis seed is one of the few that doesn't need stratification prior to seeding.

Planting depth: Surface sow

Coreopsis lancelolata L.

Little Blue Stem

Imagine open prairies with numerous species of hawks hovering above. This is the type of habitat you are likely to find little blue stem. Little bluestem is more than just a grass. It is a plant with striking burgundy fall foliage. And the seeds are a real hit with songbirds. It's a good food source and cover for various critters.

Burgundy fall foliage from this clumping plant is impressive swaying in the breeze. Ht. 1–2'.

Where to plant: Open fields, prairies, sand dunes and shores, dolomitic pavement, Jack pine plains and along the coastal Great Lakes. Hardy to zone 4.

Seed collection: Start collecting seed in September before it gets blown away in the wind. It's easiest to just cut or break off the tops of the plants and stuff them into a paper bag and clean it when you get home. The seed need only be separated from the stems, not the fuzzy petals.

Propagation: Seed and division. Cold moist stratify for one month before planting in sterile medium. I've had mixed luck with propagating this one. If having difficulty with germination, try direct seeding in the spring or fall in a restoration site or a cultivated planting bed.

Planting depth: Cover lightly.

Schizachyrium scoparium

Marsh Marigold

Aah, the Marsh Marigolds-- spring has arrived! You'll probably hear water rushing down the creeks as well when you stop to view the marsh marigolds in bloom. One of the first forest plants to flower, the marsh marigolds, aka cow slips, are a welcome site indeed in the Great Lakes region. The name "cow slip" may have come from the practice of grazing cattle on wet, waste areas where cows would often slip in the mud, or perhaps on some cow slips!

Flowers the color of egg yokes bloom first thing in the spring. Grows to 8".

Where to plant: Marsh Marigolds like it wet, which makes it a little difficult to grow in the home garden. Try planting it in a water garden where it can be suspended in a pot filled with rich, black soil. Prefers full sun. Zones 1–8.

Seed collection: The seed of marsh marigolds ripen in late spring to early summer. The seed is shed quickly, so you'll need to be on your toes to collect these. The shiny green-brown seeds are born on lengthy stems and will need to be shaken into a paper sack.

Propagation: Difficult to propagate from seed. Plant collected seed immediately in the ground after harvesting. The seed will germinate the following spring.

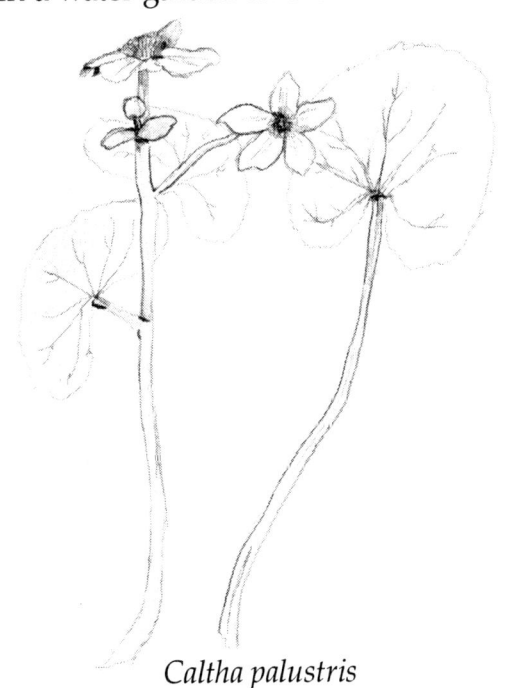

Planting depth: Just cover

Caltha palustris

Milkweed, Common

Milkweed is famously associated with monarch butterflies and what we've become to know as a remarkable feat of migration. The monarch travels thousands of miles northward from their winter resting grounds in Mexico and California expecting to be able to feed on milkweed along the way. We can help them along in their travels by planting a nice patch of native milkweed.

This summer bloomer features green and purple flowers. Ht. 2–4'.

Where to plant: Milkweed prefers full sun and will tolerate some tough soils, though they seem to grow best in sand. It is a plant that will colonize rapidly so space them at least a foot apart and allow them to fill in the spaces. A good place for these monarch attracting plants may be on the fringes of your property as the plant itself lacks an ornamental quality. Zones 3–9.

Seed collection: The seed of milkweed is probably one of the easier ones to identify and collect. They form in large pods and turn brown when ripe. Separate the cottony material from the seed as best you can and store in a dry place.

Propagation: Although easy to propagate, the milkweeds don't lend themselves well to being cramped up in flats or pots in a greenhouse. Grow in peat pots or plant as quickly as possible after they've established themselves well in the greenhouse. The other alternative of course, is to direct seed in the fall outdoors.

Asclepias syriaca

Planting depth: Just cover

New England Aster

New England aster is a good one to plant if you're looking for a late summer flower show. It was once used to relieve pain and treat diarrhea and fever. It will fill spaces in your natural landscape well and attract beneficial critters.

Lavender-pink flowers bloom late summer and into fall. Ht. 3–7'.

Where to plant: New England aster prefers moist areas that are found in many areas in the Great Lakes region, although I have observed it in drier upland areas as well. It is adaptable to most soil types. Hardy to zone 4.

Seed collection: Seed ripens in late September to October. Easy to collect in paper bags.

Propagation: Most of the asters are easy to propagate from seed. A 2–4 week cold stratification period will ensure successful germination.

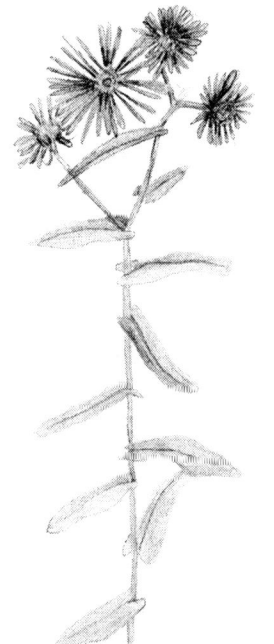

Planting depth: Just cover

Aster novae-angliae L.

Pearly Everlasting

Pearly everlasting makes a great addition to a butterfly garden. This native wildflower will attract fritillary butterflies and other species of our colorful friends. Its fuzzy white flowers with the yellow "eyes" make it a good addition to a cut flower arrangement as well. Hang a bunch upside down in an airy place to preserve for use in a dried flower arrangement.

Clustery white flowers are perfect for cut flowers. Blooms in summer. Ht. to 3'.

Where to plant: Look for pearly everlasting along roadsides and railroads. Also can be found in open, dry prairies. Plant in open, mostly sandy sites. Hardy to zone 4.

Seed collection: Seed is an achene and is harvested from late August to September. Seed is tiny and need not be separated from the fuzzy petals.

Propagation: Stratify in a cool, moist medium in a refrigerator at 35–45 degrees for one to two months. Direct seed in the spring or in a sunny greenhouse at 66–68 degrees.

Planting depth: Just cover

Anaphalis margaritacea L.

Purple Meadow-Rue

This shrubby appearing wildflower is conspicuous in my front yard perennial bed. How it got there, perhaps only the birds know for sure. Purple meadow-rue, with the delicate white flowers, will really stand out as well as fill in a large perennial flower bed. It flowers from May to July. Very hardy.

Small white flowers bloom in mid-summer. Ht. to 4'.

Where to plant: It prefers low, moist areas. Hardy to zone 4.

Seed collection: The seeds are produced in pods and can be picked from late summer onward. Seed need not be cleaned.

Propagation: Stratify seed in a moist mixture of perlite or vermiculite for up to two months in a cool, dry environment.

Planting depth: 1/8".

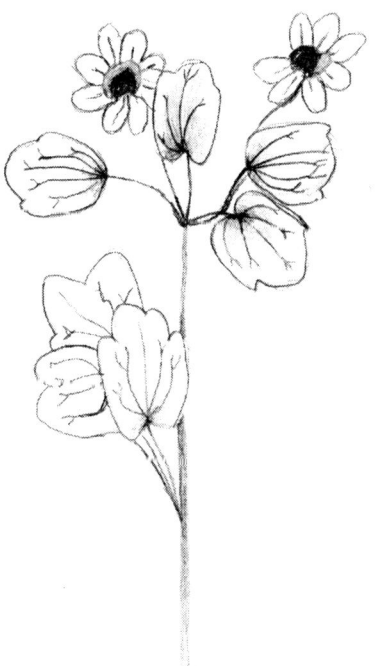

Thalictrum dasycarpum

Sweet Grass

Sweet Grass, aka holygrass, has been used by Native Americans of the Upper Midwest for incense, basket weaving and ceremonial purposes for centuries. It is an easy-to-grow plant from seed or by division of the crown.

This short statured plant is grown mostly for ceremonial purposes. Ht. to 18".

Where to plant: Appears along edges of woods, meadows, shores and boggy locations. Spreads easily. Hardy to zone 4.

Seed collection: Collect seed from July to August. Sweet grass is not a prolific producer of seed and there is a reported shortage of plants in the wild, so make sure you use the seed you harvest.

Propagation: Hand strip the seed heads but do not clean. Stratify for at least one month. Sweet grass seed can be difficult to germinate. However, once established, it produces thick roots which can be easily divided into several smaller plants.

Planting depth: Cover lightly

Hierochloe odorata

5: Starting Selected Wildflowers from Seed

Turtlehead

Here is an excellent plant to include in a water garden. Turtlehead likes it wet, but not overly so. While not invasive, it does have a spreading habit that helps it hold its own among other plants in the wild.

White blooms appear from late summer into fall. Ht. 2–3'.

Where to plant: Plant turtlehead in partial shade in moist meadows, the water's edge and borders. Zones 3–9.

Seed collection: Look for thin papery brown seeds in large pointed capsules late in the season. Harvest the seed from brown capsules by shaking out the seed over newspaper.

Propagation: A one-month cold stratification period may be needed for turtlehead to germinate. Stem cuttings taken in early spring root easily.

Planting depth: Cover lightly

Chelone glabra

White Baneberry

The striking red berries of white baneberry, also known as doll's eyes, should be reason enough to add this wildflower to your collection. Just remember, the fruit is poisonous. Native Americans reportedly drank a tea made from the root of this plant after childbirth. White baneberry is typically found in the understory of the woodland environment.

The flowers are white and bloom in early summer. Ht. from 1–3'.

Where to plant: Plant baneberry in wooded areas or adjacent to your home, cottage, or cabin. Plant among native trees and shrubs. Mass together for visual effect. Hardy to zone 4.

Seed collection: Four to eight seeds are encased in the berry so you'll have to separate the seed from the pulp. Soaking the seed for 24 hours will allow the remaining pulp to be removed a little easier.

Propagation: The seed of white baneberry can be direct seeded immediately after it has been removed from the berry. The following spring you may experience nearly 100% germination. Otherwise, it can be cleaned, dried and stored until you're ready to sow it in late winter in a greenhouse or in the spring in a grow house. For late winter or spring sowing, provide a one month cold, moist stratification. Dried seed may take a full year to germinate in pots.

Actaea alba

Planting depth: ¼".

YELLOW AVENS (GEUM)

Yellow Avens maintains a rather low profile, that is, unless you brush up against the long styles that tend to stick to everything it comes in contact with, especially your clothes. The yellow flowers are pretty though and the foliage is coarse but interesting. It is also easy to grow.

Golden yellow flowers bloom most of the summer. Ht. from 1–4''

Where to plant: Yellow avens grow in swamps, thickets and wet meadows but also does just fine in sandy upland soils, such as in a flower garden. Hardy to zone 4.

Seed collection: Seed matures in late summer.

Propagation: Stratify in a cool, moist medium for one month, then seed in flats in a greenhouse or direct seed outside.

Planting depth: Lightly cover

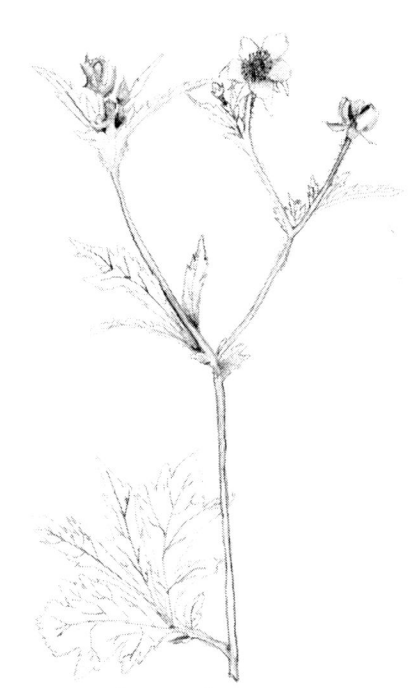

Geum aleppicum

Author's note: all of the illustrations in this chapter were done by Patrick Rambo.

References

Cullina, William, *The New England Wild Flower Society Guide to Growing and Propagating Wildflowers of the United States and Canada*, (New England Wildflower Society), Houghton Mifflin Harcourt, Boston: 2000.

Michigan Wildflowers, Harry C. Lund, Thurder Bay Press, Charlotte, NC: 8th printing, 1999.

Powell, Eileen, *Seed to Bloom: How to Grow over 500 Annuals, Perennials & Herbs*, North Adams, MA: Storey Books, 1995.

Protocol Information. Hiawatha National Forest Native Plant Program, USFS.

Schinkel, Dick and David Mohrhardt. *Favorite Wildflowers of the Great Lakes and Northeastern U.S.* David. Thunder Bay Press, Charlotte, NC: 1994.

6

OTHER PLANT PROPAGATION METHODS

One of the more rewarding gardening activities I enjoy is adding to my plant collection without spending money. One way, of course, to do this is to plant the seed we collect from our favorite plants. Botanists refer to this as sexual propagation. This aspect of propagation is covered in the chapter on germination. In this chapter I'll explain the techniques of asexual propagation. There are several asexual propagation techniques we can use to add to our collection of native plants. The asexual propagation techniques I'll cover in this chapter include stem cuttings, division, and separation.

The reasons to propagate asexually are many. Asexual propagation effectively clones a plant. We can obtain an exact duplicate of a plant by asexual propagation methods, which we can't always do by replanting collected seed, particularly in the case of replanting the seeds from a hybrid. It is also a good method to use when it's difficult to obtain the seed of a cherished plant or a certain species is difficult to germinate. A good example of a difficult wildflower to germinate (mostly because it takes so long) is blue cohosh. And like with planting collected seed, we can save money by propagating

By stepping out of your comfort zone and trying some of these easy methods of propagation, you can multiply your plant collection in no time.

plants asexually. And lastly, it is a faster way, in most cases, to produce a sizable plant than from seed.

Stem Cuttings

Propagation by stem cuttings is probably the easiest form of asexual propagation. A stem cutting can be taken from our favorite native plant and we'll have a new one in a matter of weeks. Softwood cuttings are taken from the terminal ends of herbaceous native plants—such as blue vervain, jewelweed, and blazing star when in active growth in the spring and early summer.

> **Softwood cuttings are taken from the terminal ends of the plant, in the spring or early summer of the year.**

Take cuttings from native plants in the morning, if possible, when the stems are turgid (full of water). You can cut stems with multiple nodes (a node is explained below) and then prepare them for "sticking" when you get back home or to a greenhouse. Clip several terminal stems with a sharp pair of scissors and wrap them in moist newspaper. Place the wrapped cuttings in a plastic bag and seal it. Try to keep the bag in a cool spot out of the sun until you get to where you're going.

To perform a softwood stem cutting, remove a three- to four-inch portion of the stem. Make sure to leave a couple sets of leaves which will become the growing point for the roots (hang in there, I'll explain this below). Remove the lower leaves at the point where they connect to the stem (or axis). These will become the node, or growing point, for the new plant. The upper leaves (two to three is all that is needed) will be needed to carry out photosynthesis. Dust the node with rooting powder (indolebutyric acid), which can be obtained from the houseplant section of a department store or garden center.

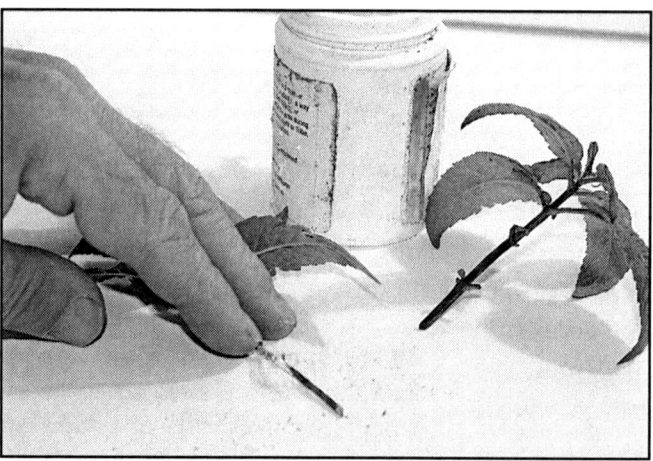

The first step in performing a stem cutting is to pluck the lower leaves, exposing the node; apply rooting hormone to the node.

Prepare a moist germination medium by mixing three parts germination mix with one part water in a large bucket or wheel barrel. Firmly pack the medium in three-inch pots or deep-cell packs. Dust the node area of the stem (where you just clipped off the leaf and petiole) with the rooting hormone. Loosen the potting medium in the center of the pot or cell in preparation for sticking the cutting. Insert the cutting in the pot so that the node is buried at least an inch deep. Firm the soil around the cutting with your fingers.

The ideal place to root cuttings is in a commercial greenhouse where temperature, humidity, and airflow can be precisely controlled. If you do this in your home, or a hobby greenhouse, keep in mind that these cuttings will need similar conditions too root as found in a commercial greenhouse.

Use a flat stick to prepare a hole to "stick" the cutting in the sterile medium.

Stick the cutting in the prepared hole, then firm soil around the buried stem.

To successfully root cuttings in your home, it will be necessary to increase humidity and keep the cuttings at a consistent temperature (70-80 degrees) and out of direct sunlight. This can be achieved by placing the cuttings under a grow light with florescent tubes or a halide bulb. The desired humidity can be maintained by placing a clear plastic dome over the cuttings and spraying a fine mist of warm water over them two to three times per day. This should be sufficient to root herbaceous cuttings.

Keep the medium moist and continue misting the leaves of the cuttings until rooting takes place. Depending on the particular plant, it should be rooted in two to six weeks. Once it is rooted, carefully remove the cuttings and pot them up like you would a houseplant or young seedling. Start watering like you would for most seedlings. That is, water well and then let it dry out somewhat before you water it again. This will encourage good root development. You can further encourage healthy roots by adding a fertilizer, organic or inorganic, with a high phosphorous content.

Division and Separation
Chances are you've performed a plant division or separation, but didn't give it a name. Division is simply dividing a perennial plant to make more plants. Here are a few suggestions to ensure success with this easy propagation technique:

- division can be done on any perennial, at any time during the growing season, though spring and fall are the best when the weather is cool and moist. Always water-in transplants. If you do a division during the summer months, be sure to give the plants a good soaking once per week;
- division is best done when the weather is still cool and wet, such as in the spring or early fall. This way, you don't have to spend time watering and your success rate will be much higher;
- choose plants that have a fibrous root, rather than a tap root. Plants with a tap root, such as the mallow species, do not take to division very well;
- don't be afraid to slice through the root systems of fibrous plants. They'll recover in no time.

Separation is simply separating a bulb or corm from a plant and replanting it. This technique is best done in the fall when the bulb has already regenerated itself through the summer. Simply separate the bulblets or cormels from the parent and replant them outside in the desired location.

And that's all there is to it. By stepping out of your comfort zone and trying some of these easy methods of propagation, you can multiply your collection in no time. Use your new starts to naturalize areas in your yard, to create a meadow, or for use in a restoration project, such as a dune along the Great Lakes.

References

Riley, Edward H. and Carroll L. Shry Jr. *Introductory Horticulture*. 6th ed. Albony, NY: Delmar-Thomson Learning, 2002.

Smith, Miranda Smith, *The Plant Propagator's Bible: A Step-by-Step Guide to Propagating Every Plant in Your Garden*, Emmaus. PA: Rodale Inc., 2007.

7

A FEW TIPS ON SOIL

"There are two kinds of soil up here," a fellow from Marquette, in Michigan's Upper Peninsula once told me, "sand and rock." This may be true in a cynical sense, yet many, wild plants flourish in and around Marquette as well as some other "geographically challenged" areas around the Great Lakes.

Fortunately, native plants will grow just fine in some seemingly intolerable situations. One example is the shallow soils of what is called an alvar out on Drummond Island, in the Eastern Upper Peninsula of Michigan. An alvar like this one consists of a thin layer of soil over limestone rock. While only a few inches deep, the alvar supports some interesting species of wildflowers, including Ram's Head, Lady's Slipper Orchid and Prairie Smoke.

So with this in mind, you should do just fine establishing wildflowers just about anywhere, including around a cabin or cottage where the soil is sandy or otherwise unsuitable for a conventional flowerbed. In other words, there is no need to haul compost and topsoil to the cabin on the weekends, like you would for domestic flowers, to improve your soil if you're planting native wildflowers.

> **There is no need to haul compost and topsoil to the cabin on the weekends, like you would for domestic flowers, to improve your soil if you're planting native wildflowers.**

Having said this, we may at times need to alter the soil conditions to accommodate certain native plants, such as in the case of restoring a dune, wetland or woodland area. If you have a basic understanding of soil you should be able to match particular wildflowers to a given site as mentioned above, or when necessary, change the soil type to accommodate different species of native plants.

A Few Words About Soil

Soil is classified into three types: clay, sand and sandy loam. Sand has the largest particles and pore spaces, thus it drains well, but also dries out rather quickly. Clay, on the other hand, has the smallest particles and is very moisture retentive. As many of you clay busters know, clay retains water to a point and then dries as hard as a rock. Have you ever tried to till the stuff?

A sandy loam soil is one containing equal parts sand, silt and clay. It absorbs moisture well and drains equally as well. Farmers and vegetable gardeners love the quality of a sandy-loam soil. In low-lying areas where I live, the cool, wet soil warms up slowly in the spring, delaying planting somewhat. Native species of wildflowers, such as Joe-pye weed, vervain and blood root love my damp, loamy soil…as does the invasive *Phragmites* that thrives in a wetland area near my house!

At times we may want to introduce some plants into our gardens that won't thrive in the existing native soils. You can amend the existing soil by adding, for instance, sand to a loamy soil to make it more suitable for woodland plants such as bunchberry and starflower. If you want to improve the ability of the soil to retain water add amendments such as

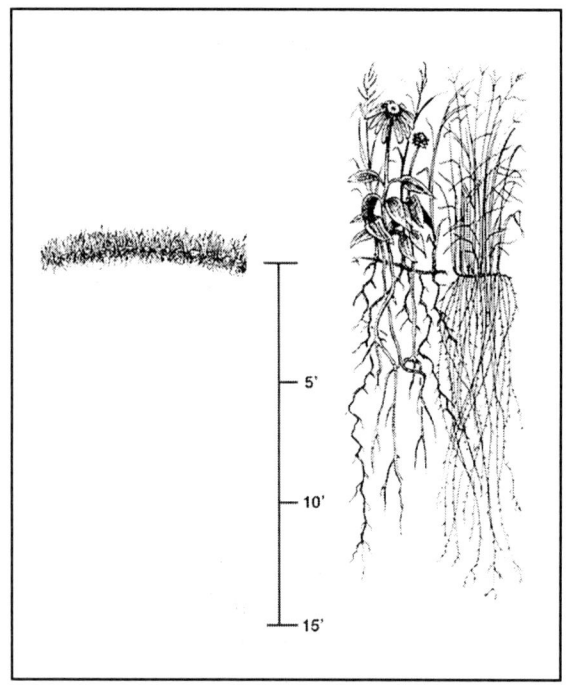

Deep-rooted native plants can prevent soil erosion. Note the difference between the roots of native plants and turf grass.
Illustration courtesy of Heidi Natura and Living Habitats.

compost and well- rotted manure. Ironically, the same organic material can be added to a clay soil to make it drain better.

Some native plants have specific pH needs. Soil pH is a measure of a soil's acidity or alkalinity. This can be crucial plants, such as bunchberry, that requires an acid soil, and many other wildflowers found in woodland areas. This is one reason it is difficult to transplant wild species to cultivated areas.

Most plants grow in a neutral soil of around 6.5–7.0. To lower the soil pH and make it more acidic, add sulfur; to raise the soil pH, add lime.

Quite frankly, I could write a book on soil alone (that is, if I were a soil scientist). Hopefully, the above information on soil will give you enough information to successfully establish wildflowers in your flowerbeds and other settings.

References

Moran, Neil. *North Country Gardening: Simple Secrets to Successful Northern Gardening.* Marquette, MI: Avery Color Studios, 2nd ed. 1997.

Riley, Edward H. and Carroll L. Shry Jr. *Introductory Horticulture.* 6th ed. Albony, NY: Delmar-Thomson Learning, 2002.

8

Creating a Wildlife Oasis

Imagine your backyard, not as a collection of various plants, but as an oasis for wildlife—birds, butterflies, hummingbirds, and perhaps a few surprise visitors, such as frogs, a rare bird, or even a bunny rabbit. Imagine pollinating insects and other beneficial bugs flitting from flower to flower, or preying on the insects that are desiccating your rose bush or potato plants.

This is what my wife and I and many others have created by letting our hair down a little and planting a nice variety of native plants. We added a couple of water features to further attract wildlife. This approach to landscaping may look a little unkempt around the edges, but it sure attracts wildlife, and provides us with hours of enjoyment.

Lord knows the critters need our help as they're pushed towards being endangered and even extinct by loss of habitat, which is the number one factor

Your yard can be certified as a wildlife habitat (see Appendix A).

> "Small 'islands' of habitat can provide food resources for birds, particularly during migration."
> Victoria D. Piaskowski, International Coordinator, Birds without Borders, Zoological Society of Milwaukee

for the decline in wildlife. Another factor contributing to this decline is pesticide use. Though all animals need our help, bees and other insects that pollinate our fruit and vegetable crops really need our assistance, as development and the use of pesticides contribute to their declining numbers. And lastly, although it is a good thing to provide sunflower seeds in a bird feeder, it is even better to offer a constant food source from native plants. In fact, some birds don't rely on feeders at all, insisting instead on foraging in the wild.

In recent years populations of nonnative honey bees have dwindled due to what some deem a "mysterious condition"—Colony Collapse Disorder. It's not really mysterious at all. It appears evident now that the bees are perishing due to the overuse of chemical pesticides and the fact that they are simply being worked to death. As native plant enthusiasts we can be a part of the solution to this problem by planting large and small plots of wildflowers as described in this book. This won't save the commercial honey bees, but rather encourage native bees and other insect pollinators.

Folks who plant wildflowers on their property won't need to visit a butterfly house to experience the beauty of butterflies. There are many species of wildflowers that attract a multitude of butterflies. By planting wildflowers for the butterflies, we can offer them four things: a source of nectar, a place to lay their eggs, food for developing butterfly larvae, and a place for them to form a butterfly chrysalis. Here is a list of wildflowers and what you can expect to attract to your property by planting them on your property.

> "Native plants, which have co-evolved with native wild birds, are more likely to provide a mix of foods—just the right kind of nutrition—and just when the birds need them."
> Stephen Kress, National Audubon Society

Native Plants That Attract Butterflies

Annise hyssop (*Agastache foeniculum*)
Nodding wild onion (*Allium cernuum*)
Butterfly weed (*Asclepias turberosa*)
Smooth aster (*Aster laevis*)
New England aster (*Aster novae-angliae*)
Sand cororeopsis (*Coreopsis lanceolata*)
Prairie coreopsis (*Coreopsis palmata*)
Pale purple coneflower (*Echinacea pallida*)
Purple coneflower (*Echinacea purpurea*)
Fireweed (*Epilobium augustifolium*)
Rattlesnake master (*Eryngium yuccifulium*)
Boneset (*Eupatorium perfoliatum*)
Queen of the prairie (*Filipendulla rubra*)
Prairie smoke (*Geum triflorum*)
Downy sunflower (*Helianthus mollis*)
Western sunflower (*Helianthus occidentalis*)
Meadow blazing star (*Liatris ligulistylis*)
Prairie blazing star (*Liatris pycnostachya*)
Wild lupine (*Lupinus perennis*)
Foxglove penstemon (*Penstemon digitalis*)
Large-flowered beardtongue (*Penstemon grandiflorus*)
Yellow coneflower (*Ratibida pinnata*)
Blackeyed Susans (*Rubeckia hirta*)
Stiff goldenrod (*Solidago rigida*)

North Country Gardening with Wildflowers

Plants That Attract Hummingbirds

Columbine (*Aquilegia canadensis*)
Milkweed (*Asclepias syriaca*)
New England asters (*Aster novae-angliae* L.)
Purple coneflower (*Echinacea purpurea*)
Rough blazing star (*Liatris aspera*)
Cardinal flower (*Lobelia cardinalis*)
Rough blazing star (*Liatris aspera*)
Obedient plant (*Physostegia virginiana*)
Monarda (*Monarda fistulosa* L.)
Goldenrod *(Salidago canadensis)*

References

Hair, Marty. *Going Native.* Detroit Free Press, July 31, 2001.

Nowak, Mariette. *Birdscaping in the Midwest: A Guide to Gardening with Native Plants to Attract Birds.* Blue Mound, WI: Itchy Cat Press, 2007.

9

Keep It Natural: Landscaping with Wildflowers

Each year I spend less time on the lawn mower and more time admiring the wild plants and wildlife around my yard. I enjoy observing the subtle and not-so-subtle changes in my perennial wildflowers during the season. And on any given summer day you can see rabbits, squirrels, hummingbirds, various butterflies, and even frogs in and near my yard. That's because my yard contains a diversity of plants, mostly native to the area. It might not be the perfectly manicured and landscaped lawn, but it surely benefits wildlife and, in turn, provides hours of enjoyment for my wife and me.

> **A good place to start with native plants is to plant a few in your existing flower bed.**

Just think, you can have all of this and save time and money and help the environment by reducing or eliminating mowing, fertilizing, and spraying harmful chemicals on your lawn.

Planting native flowers can be as simple as making room for a few perennial wildflowers and grasses in a flower bed—to restoring a complex wetland habitat. In this chapter I'll introduce the principles of landscape design and how they

can be applied when landscaping with native wildflowers. I'll also give you a few options for preparing a site for planting, including:
1. removing the soil with a sod cutter;
2. applying a chemical or nonchemical fertilizer;
3. cultivating with a roto-tiller or farm implement;
4. smothering the site with a tarp.

If you're still with me after reading about site preparation I'll go on to explain how to establish a seed bed with native wildflowers and walk you through the various planting scenarios you may encounter, including:
1. adding a few wildflowers to a flower bed
2. converting an entire lawn to wildflowers
3. installing a buffer along the shoreline of a lake or river
4. creating a woodland garden
5. creating a meadow or prairie

Landscaping the Natural Way

Like any type of landscaping, we should follow some simple rules of landscape design when planting wildflowers-- that is, if we want it to look like more than just a smattering of wildflowers. However, in the case of landscaping with native plants we are also trying to create a natural look, one like you would find in nature. I think it is possible to apply the principles of ornamental landscaping to landscaping with native wildflowers by bearing in mind how plants would look in nature. Although we may be inclined to think that plants occur at random in nature, a closer look will convince you otherwise.

Woman planting wildflower "plugs" along roadside. (Photo courtesy of Prairie Nursery, Westfield, WI)

If you can follow the principles of landscape design as explained below, with an eye toward how plants naturally occur in the wild,

I promise you can create an effective, beautiful landscape even if you lack an artistic flair.

Focalization. This refers to establishing a focal point that draws the eye into the landscape. With a wildflower planting, the focal point is probably going to be a mass of showy wildflowers such as purple coneflower or coreopsis. A focal point is usually located where it can be viewed from a window, deck, patio, or sidewalk.

Rhythm and line. Refers to the way the wildflower planting flows. It could refer to a winding or wavy pattern of a border (as opposed to a square or rectangular pattern with stiff, right angles) or the way the flowers themselves spill through the landscape. It also refers to how elements in a landscape are tied together or how they flow from one point to another. In a traditional landscape, it is attributed to how one flower is visually connected to another. For instance, plants of similar height, color and texture will flow together better than plants that aren't as visually compatible.

> **If purchasing plants from a nursery, it is preferable to use plants native to your specific area; this will help preserve the genotype or heritage of the seed.**

Rhythm and line can also refer to how the plants themselves create different shapes, lines, and even angles by the way they're positioned in the landscape. A good way to get an idea of how to landscape for nature is to take a leisurely walk in the woods and observe how rhythm and line is achieved by mother nature.

Scale and proportion. This landscape principle takes into account the height of each plant in relationship to the size of competing physical structures and even of other plants in the landscape. For example, plants should not tower over a split rail fence you've installed in a corner in your yard, nor should short plants be planted near the foundation of a home, where they will be dwarfed by the size of this structure.

An example of scale and proportion with native plants is when smaller plants are placed around rock or stone, similar to what you would see in nature. Taller plants would be more likely to be in open, sunny locations.

Balance. A landscape is in balance if each side of a visual plane carries equal weight. For instance, if you were to devote your front yard to all native wildflowers and a sidewalk ran up the middle to your door, the plants on either side

> **Don't be surprised if the native plants in your perennial bed do better than their domestic counterparts, in terms of hardiness and ease of growth.**

would be equal in terms of height, spread, and number. In formal landscaping, symmetry would come into play, which means each side as mentioned above would be a duplicate of the other. Native landscapes, although balanced, are more likely to be asymmetrical rather than symmetrical.

Simplicity. This principle is just how it sounds. Keep it simple. Use a limited variety of native plants, massed together as appropriate, to make a lasting impression. Even in nature you'll see that there are a limited number of different plants in a given area.

Preparing the Site for a Wildflower Planting

The Sod Cutter Method

A sod cutter will effectively remove the sod. This cutter can be of the manual type that will give you quite a workout (not to mention shortness of breath and a sore back), or the power type that can be acquired from a rental store. Providing the soil doesn't need amending, it can then be shallow-cultivated with a roto-tiller to scuff up the soil for seeding, unless you're planting plugs or mature plants, in which case it can be left alone until you plant your plants.

Applying a Non-selective Herbicide

A nonselective herbicide containing glyphosate will kill all of the existing vegetation. RoundUp is probably the most popular of the glyphosate herbicides. It has a short residual life, that is, it breaks down quickly in the environment. However, if you decide to go this route, be sure to read the product label carefully and wear the appropriate safety equipment when using it.

A nontoxic alternative to glyphosate is a horticulture vinegar-based solution sold by several horticulture supply companies (the vinegar in your pantry will also kill weeds). Herbicides should be applied on a warm (at least 60 degrees), dry day. It will take on average about ten days to kill the existing vegetation with an herbicide, after which time you can either cultivate the area and seed, as detailed below, or plant the plugs and then mulch with four inches of bark, straw, or pine needle mulch.

A Season of Cultivation
It is also possible to simply cultivate the area for an entire season, which will effectively kill off the existing vegetation and provide loose soil for planting. This method will also bring weed seeds to the surface, which, I promise, will eventually sprout and try to sabotage your efforts. If you resort to this method of weed eradication it is suggested you start plowing in the spring and then plow and disk or cultivate with a tiller every two weeks to eliminate all roots. Two weeks later switch to shallow cultivation to eliminate emerging seedlings from those seeds that have been churned up to the surface by cultivation. Cultivate in this way right up until fall, when you could actually start planting. Otherwise, wait until spring to sow the (stratified) seed directly into the ground.

Farmers often use a combination of methods to prepare the ground for planting, including the application of an herbicide on a warm, sunny day in early fall, followed-up by plowing and disking a few times; it is then set to plant in the spring. However, with native plants, a spring planting won't be possible, unless you stratify the seed as explained in this book. The other option would be to sow them in the late fall, which will allow for a natural stratification period over the winter. Otherwise, you can start them in a greenhouse and set them out as plugs in the spring is likewise detailed in this book.

> **Note:** Old pastures will need to be plowed and disked, rather than roto-tilled to break through what is an almost impenetrable layer of thatch that builds up.

Smother Those Weeds!
The last method I want to mention requires no chemicals or fossil fuels at all. A plastic tarp or two layers of heavy cardboard can be laid over an area for an entire season. This will kill the vegetation and make it ready to plant the following year either by seed or with plugs. The tarp needs to be opaque and properly staked so it doesn't blow away. Keep the cardboard in place by covering with compost or rotted cow manure. After the vegetation is killed off the ground can be shallow-cultivated in preparation for seeding or plugging.

Weed control is going to be an issue regardless of what method you use to establish native plants.

Establishing a Seed Bed

The seeding of native plants is best done by hand, since the fluffy petals in some native seed will clog most mechanical seed spreaders (having said this, there is a special type of no-drill seed planter for native plants; check with your local soil conservation district to see if they have one).

There are two opportune times to sow native seed: fall and spring. Seed sown in the fall will undergo a natural stratification period over the winter. Spring-sown seeds must be from wildflower seed that has been stratified per the instructions in this book.

One advantage of seeding by hand is that you can better dictate what seed is planted in individual areas in your yard. For instance, you could have a mix for full sun, full shade, or partial shade. Another mix could be of your favorite native plants that you want to plant in a specific area, for instance so they can be viewed from a window, deck, or patio. Mix the seed with sand, peat moss, and/or vermiculite to make it a little easier to distribute. Be sure to thoroughly distribute the seed in the seed bed.

Weed control is going to be an issue regardless of what method you use to establish native plants. It will be fairly easy to mulch around plugs or mature plants that are spaced up to a foot apart. However, if you are establishing native plants from seed you will need to manually pull or, better yet, cut the weeds at the crown (this avoids disturbing the soil where more weeds will sprout) as they pop up between your seeded wildflowers. This little ritual will need to be performed until the plants start to establish themselves in two to three years.

A clump of coreopsis looks natural planted in front of this rock.

Using Wildflowers in the Landscape
Adding Native Plants to a Flower Bed

A good way to start with native plants is to plant a few in an existing flower bed. Like any perennial plants, wildflowers need to be started either as transplants in a greenhouse (rather than direct seeding) or as potted perennials bought from a nursery. When purchasing plants from a nursery, it is preferable to use plants native to your specific area. This will help preserve the genotype or heritage of the seed. In other words, a true native plant is one grown from locally harvested seed.

Transplant native plants in the early spring or fall of the year. If you plant during the summer, be sure to provide at least one inch of water per week to help establish healthy native plants. Prepare a spot for native plants like you would for any other perennial. In most cases, native plants do well in loose soil rich in organic matter, though they will also do well in some stubborn sand and clay soil. Generally speaking, they do best in the soil they're accustomed to in their native habitat.

Mature, native wildflowers are planted like any other perennial plant. That is, dig a hole slightly wider and deeper than the size of the root system. This is the time to add any soil amendments you deem necessary, such as compost, sand, or a mixture of sand, silt, and clay (i.e., loam). Always provide an initial "watering in" of any perennial plants by pouring water right into the hole you've dug before backfilling it.

Group several native plants together in a flower bed to make them more noticeable. Massing them together will also attract butterflies, pollinating insects, and perhaps even a hummingbird or two. I like to group at least three plants of the same type together in a flower bed, but there is no limit to how many you can mass together. As with any perennial plants, you can color coordinate your flowers and mix in plants with a coarse texture to contrast them with plants with a fine texture. For instance, try combining plants such as Joe-pye weed, which has a coarse texture, with a fine textured grass, such as little bluestem.

Don't be surprised if the native plants in your perennial bed do better than their domestic counterparts, in terms of hardiness and ease of growth. There is no need to pamper native plants with fertilizers or run up the water bill watering them once they're established. In my experience, native plants just seem much more adaptable than so-called exotic plants, some of which trace their origins to South America and Africa.

Lastly, plant according to the individual needs for sun, partial shade, and full shade. Assuming that your existing perennial bed has been amended with some type of organic matter and/or topsoil, there should be no need to make any radical changes to your soil. Fertilizing with inorganic fertilizers isn't necessary or recommended. Slow-release organic fertilizers and/or compost are much better alternatives.

> **A good way to get an idea of how to landscape for nature is to take a leisurely walk in the woods and observe how rhythm and line is achieved by mother nature.**

Once you've incorporated some native plants into your flower beds, you may be tempted to devote a larger portion of your lawn to native plants and do away with or limit the use of that polluting, fossil-burning, noisy lawn mower. Go for it! In the next section, learn how to "get wild" with native plants and kick the time-honored but environmentally harmful habit of maintaining the perfect (perfectly boring!) all-American lawn.

Going Wild with Wildflowers
(Converting a lawn to all wildflowers)

Unless you're simply adding a few perennials wildflowers to an existing bed (as explained below), you'll have to spend a considerable amount of prep time to convert an entire lawn to wildflowers. In so doing, you will want to design something that looks pretty natural, in other words, something that looks like a meadow or other wild area.

As with any planting project where there is a lawn involved, you will need to remove the turf. Do this in such a way as to not awaken the dormant weed seed lying just below the surface (actually, there may be seeds of native plants in the soil, but for our purposes we can't take the chance).

For obvious reasons you will not be burning the ground cover around your home. The use of an herbicide may be considered; however, make sure to check to see if there are any restrictions on the use of a chemical herbicide in your city, township, or county. Alternatives, such as horticultural vinegar can be considered.

The planting of wildflowers in a lawn can proceed per the instructions in this book, i.e., from plugs, potted plants or by seed.

9: Keep it Natural: Landscaping with Wildflowers

How your wildflowers look in the home landscape may come into play, and will certainly become an issue with your neighbors. This is when you will need to follow the suggestions above regarding landscape design (focalization, balance, etc.). What works particularly well around a home is to mass the flowers in different locations. This really draws the eye in and more closely replicates nature.

I've heard two suggestions when it comes to converting a lawn into wildflowers. One is to place a sign in a prominent place in your lawn, indicating that the plants in your yard isn't a collection of weeds, but a planned attack on the status quo of the perfect green lawn, or some such language. Another suggestion is to keep a strip of lawn mowed near the sidewalk. This will keep things tidy and perhaps pacify the neighbors who can't see the wisdom in what you're doing.

A Shoreline Planting

For the next three planting scenerios (shoreline, woodland, prairie/meadow), you can choose to establish wildflowers either by seeding, plugs, or potted plants—which you will do by employing the methods described within the covers of this book.

There is no question that shorelines around lakes and streams are getting more and more crowded with cottages and cabins. It seems everyone wants to live on the water. Some folks bring the same landscaping thoughts to their shoreline property that they had in suburbia, i.e., creating the perfect lawn. In many cases those lawns lead right up to the shoreline. These folks may even use the same chemicals that keep their home lawns green and weed free. Unfortunately, these chemicals can eventually find their way into our pristine bodies of water, disturbing the natural ecology of the water system.

What's more, a perfectly manicured lawn right up to the water's edge looks a little out of place surrounded by all of this natural beauty. Enter native wildflowers! We can use wildflowers to work with nature, not agin' her. We can eliminate at least some of this high-maintenance lawn by establishing buffer zones that not only buffer chemical runoff, but will also halt erosion and buffer some not-so-natural views and noises we sometimes encounter on popular lakes and streams, like the Sunday afternoon jet skier or party-reveling canoeist. Lastly, with a lush planting of native plants, we can attract wildlife to the relative cover that they need to feed and nest in.

To establish a shoreline native habitat, prepare the soil as mentioned above and then search for the appropriate plants that can adapt to the moist habitats found along the water's edge. A 35-foot buffer zone (from the water's edge back) with flowing lines is recommended to blend in and look natural.

One thing that sets this project apart from some of the other native planting or restoration projects is the potential for erosion of soil during the ground preparation stages. When working up the soil right near a shoreline, work with small sections at a time and use straw and/or landscape fabric to prevent soil from eroding into the water, at least until the plants are well established. It is also beneficial to mix in small shrubs and even trees to prevent erosion. These plants can also frame a view of the water, as well as buffer those undesirable sights and sounds on the water.

Before you start altering a shoreline right near the water's edge, contact a governing agency, such as the Department of Environmental Quality (DEQ) or Department of Natural Resources, to determine if a permit is needed. For further assistance with this type of project, contact your local soil conservation district office.

Woodland Planting

Establishing a woodland habitat with wildflowers may be a bit of a challenge, but it is certainly not impossible. You will need to be more selective when choosing plants that will thrive in a woodland environment. This will include plants suitable for partial shade or full shade, and also those that may like it a little more on the acidic side. The soil in a woodland environment may also have a sandy or silty composition, another consideration when choosing native plants. I suggest you plant a woodland garden in such a way that the plants look natural in a woodland setting. You can achieve a natural look by massing plants together and properly spacing them throughout the landscape.

Native plantings like this one are important to prevent erosion and the spread of invasice plants.

In a true woodland setting you'll have to really work with mother nature. You'll be competing with the roots of trees and other native plants. Also, there may be other plants well established in the woodland area, thus you won't want to go changing the soil too much.

Potted perennial wildflowers will establish themselves quicker in a woodland setting than they would if you tried to establish them from seed. Space your plants according to recommendations. Mulch in between plants with straw, bark, pine needles, or other appropriate mulches.

Establishing a Prairie or Meadow
When it comes to viewing and enjoying the outdoors, I never used to appreciate prairies much, favoring instead to be surrounded by what I figured was the more diverse boreal forest or the serenity and beauty of the water's edge of our pristine shorelines here in the Upper Great Lakes region. One reason for this lack of appreciation was simply that prairies are in short supply. In other words, I just hadn't seen many! And it's no wonder. Currently, only about 1% of tallgrass prairie remain in the U.S., most of the rest of this acreage having been gobbled up by farm implements and residential and commercial development. In the past few years the Nature Conservancy and other conservation groups have made prairies more visible, as they seek to purchase and preserve some of these spaces where native wildflowers dominate.

When we establish a mass planting of wildflowers in our yards or acreage, we are replicating, in large part, the great prairies of our heritage. To replicate a true prairie you will need to purchase prairie seed mixes that are suitable for your soil type and climate.

To establish a prairie, use some of the methods mentioned above, such as removing sod, or try a season-long cultivation. Another way, especially for large acreage, is to burn the existing vegetation and then scuff up the surface of the ground with a disk. Make sure you have the blessing (in the way of a permit) from the local authorities before burning for any purpose.

After burning off the old vegetation, the seed is then dropped by hand or with mechanical spreaders. It will be a challenge to control the weeds that will germinate regardless of what method you use to prepare the soil. One way to deal with this on a large scale is to mow down the young forbs, or wildflowers, in the early spring with the mower deck set to about eight inches from the ground. This will at least help keep the weeds from going to seed. Eventually, the native plants will prevail.

If we remove the turf by one of the methods mentioned above, we can either use plugs, small perennial wildflower plants, or seed to establish our wildflower oasis. Purchasing inexpensive, small potted native plants is the best bet for a relatively small area (less than about 2700 sq. ft.). These plugs may be purchased through a soil conservation district office or a private garden supply store.

As you can see, this is no task for the timid. However, armed with as much knowledge as you can muster, it can be done. See sources listed in the back of this book for further information on planting wildflowers, as well as for seed suppliers in the Great Lakes region.

References:

Landscaping for Water Quality: Concepts and Garden Designs for Homeowners. Center for Environmental Study, Grand Rapids, MI. Revised: Oct. 2004.

Landscaping with Native Plants. United States Environmental Protection Agency, March 1999.

Steiner, Lynn M., *Landscaping with Native Plants of Michigan.* St. Paul, MN: Voyageur Press, 2006.

Ten Steps to Successful Small Wildflower Seeding. Wildflower Farms Seeds & Services, 2007.

10

A RAIN GARDEN OF WILDFLOWERS

If you're reading this book, I'm sure you care about the health of our lakes, rivers, streams, and the water we drink. One way we can help keep these waterways clean is to install a rain garden and fill it with native plants.

A rain garden diverts water from our rooftops that could potentially wash fertilizers, pesticides, automobile spills, and other harmful contaminants into our waterways. This can happen either directly, such as in the case of lawn chemicals from our lakeside homes washing directly into a lake, or indirectly by the water washing out onto the street and carrying contaminants to storm drains and eventually into a lake or stream. These contaminants can and do harm fish, produce excess plant growth, and poison our drinking water. In addition, siltation can be a huge problem in waterways. That is, silt is carried into our favorite fishing holes, stealing oxygen from these bodies of water where fish and invertebrates live.

Photo courtesy of Ruth Louck, Prairie Nursery of Westfield, WI

> **A rain garden is a simple, affordable thing the homeowner can do to benefit the environment.**

"It's all about preserving water quality," says Susan Letts, a landscape designer in the Harbor Springs, Michigan, area who has installed many such gardens.

A rain garden redirects the water from your roof and sends it to what is essentially a garden of native plants. From there, the water can be properly filtered and recycled. By planting a rain garden, we can do our part to preserve our precious groundwater and waterways. Rain gardens help the local ecology by:

1. keeping harmful contaminants (lawn fertilizers, salt, insecticides, oil, and other vehicle liquids) and excessive silt from entering our lakes and streams;
2. attracting wildlife—clean water and native plants are a perfect fit to attract birds, butterflies, and beneficial insects that will actually help reduce our dependence on insecticides to control problem pests;
3. allowing water to filter into the ground, which replenishes local aquifers;
4. beautifying our yards and neighborhoods;
5. eliminating puddles in our yards and, on a larger scale, flooding in our neighborhoods; and
6. diverting water, in some cases, that would otherwise end up in our crawl space or basement.

With an overflow cistern system, you can capture rain water in a 50-gallon barrel. The overflow, or excess water will end up in your garden of wildflowers.

Now that I've told you what rain gardens are, let me tell you what they're not. They are not ponds. The gardens are constructed in such a way that the water seeps into the ground without forming a swimming hole. They don't attract mosquitoes for the same reason. Any puddles you might experience would only last a few hours, at best. As for maintenance, they don't require any more maintenance than a native flower garden. The only maintenance would be in the years ahead, since the perennial wildflowers will need to be thinned out.

They also need not be weedy or messy. By following some of the design ideas you've garnered over the years and read in this book, you can build a beautiful rain garden with native plants.

And lastly, it need not be expensive. The main costs are your native plants and labor. That's why we have friends—to give us some of their extra plants and help us prepare the site! Believe me, what you spend on a rain garden will be well worth the effort.

Designing and Installing a Rain Garden

As mentioned earlier, our homes and gardens can be an extension or aid to the natural ecology around us. Unlike more expensive "green ideas," such as an expensive electric car or a windmill in your backyard, a rain garden is one of those affordable, simple things the homeowner and gardener can do to benefit the environment.

> **Rain gardens help the local ecology by attracting wildlife, and also by keeping harmful contaminants and excessive silt from entering our lakes and streams.**

A rain garden is simply a garden that catches rainwater. The ideal location for the garden is near the downspout that drains the most water from your roof. The garden should extend ten to fifteen feet from the foundation of your home, according to Letts, so that water doesn't seep into your basement or crawl space.

The best way to capture the maximum amount of water from the downspout is to bury a solid four-inch PVC pipe under the ground, going from the downspout to the upper edge of the garden. This pipe need be buried only deep enough to remain out of sight.

As with designing any flower bed, use your imagination to arrive at the shape and size you desire. These days, flower beds are typically island or kidney shaped, just to give you an idea. You can mark out the shape of the bed with a hose or rope. Now you're ready to remove the sod. This is probably the most physically challenging aspect of this project; you may wish to recruit some help with removing and hauling away the sod.

Here are some suggestions for where you should locate your rain garden:
1. in an open, mostly sunny spot where people can view your creation;
2. within sight of a window in your home and/or a deck or patio;
3. near the downspout that drains the most water; and
4. in a mostly flat area (however, it can be built on a sloping lawn, which I'll show you in the pages ahead).

Deep-rooted Plants

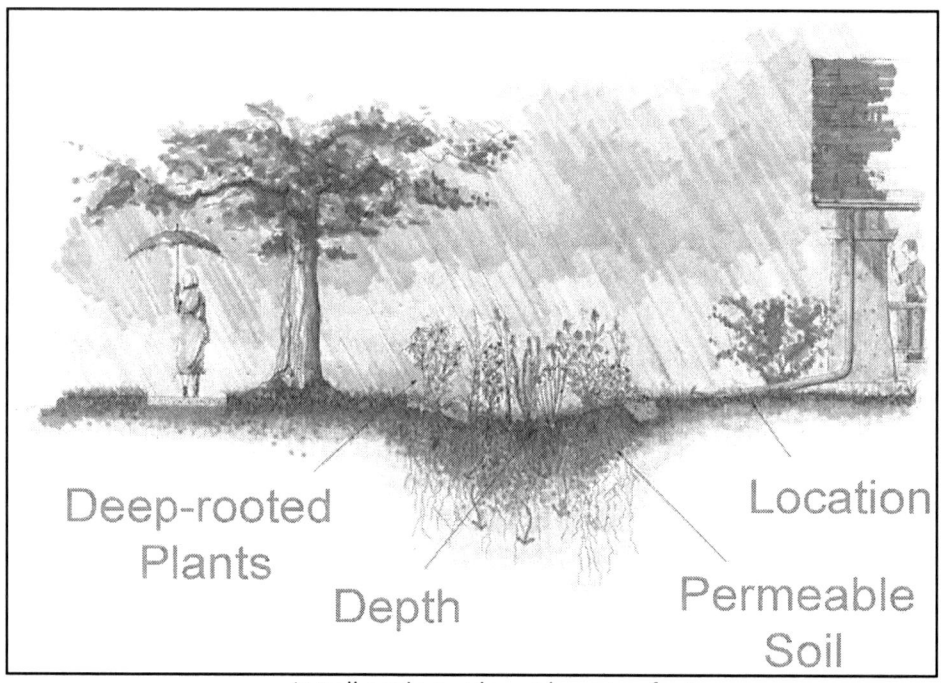

Depth

Location

Permeable Soil

Install a rain garden at least ten feet from the foundation of a home.

Like any garden, a rain garden should be located in an area that receives full sun for most of the day. Avoid situating a rain garden where there is a lot of foot traffic or need for access to utilities, etc.

The size of a rain garden varies. However, a good rule of thumb is to build it no larger than 20-30% of the area it is draining. To determine this, simply measure the length and width of your roof area and size the garden accordingly.

A rain garden should be dug four to eight inches deep in the center. This is sufficient to absorb the runoff from the roof and lawn areas. The garden for the wildflowers is dug level, like any garden, even on a sloping lawn. In the case of a sloping lawn, fill may have to be brought in to level off the garden. The fill for a rain garden should be good-quality garden soil with plenty of organic matter.

Plant a rain garden like you would any flower garden. That is, group plants together by height, color, and texture. If the bed is an island bed that is viewed from all sides, plant the tallest plants in the middle. A bed that is only viewed from one or two sides can be planted so that the tallest plants are in the back of the garden.

And that is pretty much it. This is a project any do-it-yourselfer can handle, although there are landscapers who will perform the task for you.

References:

Letts, Susan. *Landscaping for Water Quality*, DVD. Letts Landscape LLC. Harbor Springs, MI.

Rain Gardens: *A How-to Manual for Homeowners*. Wisconsin Department of Natural Resources, DNR Publication, PUB-WT-776, 2003.

11

Be on the Lookout for Invasive Species!

Understanding the devastating effects of invasive plants should give us further impetus to grow native plants. Invasive plants wreak havoc on the environment by choking out native species of plants that would have otherwise provided food and shelter to the wildlife we enjoy so much. In addition, aquatic species of invasive plants, such as Eurasian water milfoil, chokes the waterways and can restrict boat access to waterways. This devastation has implications for all of us who enjoy the outdoors: hunters, fisherman, bird watchers, and—of course—the intrepid wildflower enthusiast.

> **Invasive plants wreak havoc on the environment by choking out native species of plants that would have otherwise provided food and shelter to the wildlife we enjoy so much.**

Another example of the negative impact of invasive species is the havoc that is wreaked by a familiar plant called purple loosestrife (*Lythrum salicaria*). It has pretty purple spikes of flowers, but effectively chokes out places where fish and other wildlife would otherwise feed, seek shelter and reproduce and rear their young. Native plants, including wild rice, doesn't have a chance in these choked-out areas. Each year thousands more acres of wetlands, marshes, pastures and riparian meadows in the Great Lakes regions are taken over by invasive species; the economic impact is in the millions.

What Are Invasive Plants?

Invasive plants have been in North America since the first boat arrived in the New World. So just what is an invasive plant? Perhaps it sounds a little like something from another planet, but an invasive species, sometimes referred to as an exotic plant, is simply a nonnative plant that was either accidentally or intentionally introduced to this country from afar. What's more, for various reasons it is troublesome to the ecology. Not all imported plants are considered troublesome or invasive. For instance, Indian paintbrush (*Castilleja coccinea*) is not native to North America, yet it coexists with native species, having little, if any, negative impact on the environment.

One particular troublemaker is spotted knapweed (*Centaurea maculosa*). Although beekeepers like it for the nectar that produces tasty honey, spotted knapweed can take over acres and acres of land. And because of the chemical poison it emits, it will boot out virtually all native species in its path. Invasive species can be pesky in other ways too, such as when they overrun your favorite hiking trail, making it easy to lose the trail (not to mention that the seed clings to our clothing, further spreading to other areas). The plants can also get caught up in the chains of a mountain bike or even cause our skin to blister and discolor (which can happen with wild parsnip, *Pastinaca sativa*).

Invasive species are everywhere, like the knapweed along the road ways, the watermilfoil in the waterways and the St. John's wort along the two-tracks in the forests. Invasive plants can quickly move into sites where the soil has been disturbed by such activities as logging, development, and ATV use.

All Is Not Lost

The war on invasive species is a gargantuan one. As with the rampant rat problem in New York City, we are simply outnumbered and outsmarted by invasive plants.

Invasive species have ways to ensure their survival and rapid proliferation. For instance, garlic mustard (*Alliaria petiolata*) is an invasive species that can produce over 3,000 seeds per plant, seeds that are viable for over ten years. Other plants, such as the aforementioned spotted knapweed, are aleopathic, meaning they actually spew out a chemical poison that keeps other plants from encroaching upon them and thus ensure rapid proliferation of this plant. And like the rats that live beneath the city of New York, they may be just too difficult and expensive to eradicate.

Fortunately, there are some steps we can take to halt the spread of invasive plants. The first thing is to learn to recognize invasive species. With this knowledge, you can avoid purchasing them from garden centers. Also, give them a wide berth by walking around, not through them. Other ways include planting native plants in disturbed areas as soon as possible after it has been bulldozed over. Still other ways include ensuring that ATVs stay on designated trails and by reporting heavy infestations of troublesome invasive species to your state department or ministry of natural resources. Also, avoid removing plants and soil from wild areas and bringing it home to your flower gardens. Lastly, it helps to promptly clean the clothes and equipment that have come in contact with invasive plants.

Volunteers remove purple loosestrife from an area at the mouth of the Tahquamenon River.

Small infestations on your property can possibly be eradicated by removing the entire plant before it goes to seed. If you go this route, bear in mind that disturbing the soil where invasive species have taken over may result in more of the same, as the seeds of the same plant may take advantage of the disturbed soil. If you do decide to remove perennial invasive species, be sure to dig deep to remove all of the root system of the plant.

Here are some more options for removing or controlling invasive species:
1. smother the plants with an opaque tarp or corrugated card board. Make sure this material is staked down or otherwise secured so it doesn't blow away;

2. spray the plants with a glyphosate or vinegar-based herbicide. Be sure to read the labeling carefully to avoid off-target contamination and/or exposure to eyes, skin, etc.
3. use a root talon, a lightweight, fairly inexpensive tool, to remove shallow rooted plants. It's not suitable for thorn plants because of the hand feeding that is required. You can take a stab at the root of baby's breath, burdock and wild parsnip with any type of tool you can find that has a sharp end, such as a spud bar they use in ice fishing.
4. small infestations can be eliminate by burning individual plants with a propane torch. A fire permit may still be required. Control of baby's breath, and buckthorn have been successful; do it early in year to be most practical and effective.

Contact your local extension agent about releasing a beetle to control and out break of purple loosestrife.

Common Invasive Wildflowers in the Great Lakes Region and Potential Damage to the Environment

Purple loosestrife (*Lythrum salicaria*): infests wetlands, shorelines, wet meadows, and roadsides. Dense stands of purple loosestrife boot out native plants that would normally feed local wildlife.

Spotted knapweed (*Centaurea maculosa*): a shallow-rooted plant that actually furthers the devastating effects of erosion. It shows up everywhere, particularly on sunny, disturbed areas and along roadsides.

St. John's wort (*Hypericum perforatum* L.): another plant that offers little benefit to wildlife or the local ecology. It too shows up in areas that have been disturbed by development, clearing, etc.

Wild parsnip (*Pastinaca sativa*): can be prevalent along roadsides in good years. It also invades prairies, pine barrens, roadsides, pastures, and oak savannahs. In addition, it can become an allergen. People who brush up against the foliage can develop a sensitivity to the sun, which may result in blisters and burns.

Leafy spurge (*Euphorbia esula*): also invades open habitats like prairies, roadsides, pastures, pine barrens, and oak savannahs.

Garlic mustard (*Alliaria petiolata*): an early bloomer that will quickly shade out many of the beautiful wildflowers mentioned in this book. It shows up in undisturbed forests and along roadsides.

Other species that are bothersome for wildlife and the ecology include:

>Canada thistle (*Cirsium arvense*)
>Reed canary grass (*Phalaris arundinacea*)
>Common buckthorn (*Rhamnus cathartica*)
>Glossy buckthorn (*Rhamnus frangula*)
>Exotic bush honeysuckle (*Lonicera* spp.)
>Multiflora rose (*Rosa multiflora*)

References

A Field Identification Guide to Invasive Plants in Michigan's Natural Communities. Lansing, MI: Michigan State University Extension, 2009.

Grodde, Margaret and Strobl, Silvia. *The Trouble with Invasive Exotic Species,* Ontario Ministry of Natural Resources, n.d.

Plants Out of Place: USDA NRCS Natural Resources Conservation Service, n.d.

Why Should I Care About Native Species? Midwest Invasive Plant Network, n.d.

Purple Loosestrife: What You Should Know, What You Can Do, Ontario Federation of Anglers & Hunters, n.d.

Weed Control Methods Handbook. The Nature Conservancy, April 2001.

GLOSSARY

FOR YOUR UNDERSTANDING

Annual: a plant that completes its life cycle in one year. Annuals are started from seed in the spring and grow, flower, produce seeds, and then die in one year.

Bulb: an underground plant structure, such as a lily bulb, consisting of scales that can be separated and used to propagate the plant.

Chaff: what's left over after cleaning seed.

Corm: a swollen underground portion of the stem of a plant. Corms usually grow cormels, which can be separated from the main corm and planted to add to your collection of a particular plant.

Cutting: a portion of a plant, usually terminal, taken to propagate the species. A cutting usually consists of two to three leaves and at least one node (see **node** below).

Dehisce: the act of a seed pod opening spontaneously when the seed ripens. Often, this means it is difficult to capture the seed because it immediately ejects from the pod after ripening and gets carried away on the wind or by animals.

Division: a form of asexual propagation where the plant is divided to form a new plant by pulling or cutting the root system into at least two sections.

Ecosystem: an association of plants and animals adapted to particular soil, light, moisture, and climate conditions.

Exotic plant: a plant introduced in North America with the onset of European settlement.

Focalization: the focal point in a landscape. This is an area that stands out from the rest of the landscape. The focal point in a wildflower planting could be a grouping of bold and colorful flowers, such as purple coneflower or cardinal flower.

Forb: an herbaceous, broadleaf plant (not grass) often used in association with prairies. Forb is synonymous with wildflower.

Fruit: the covering for a seed or seeds.

Genotype: a class of native plants specific to a location. For instance, blackeyed Susan seed collected in Door County, Wisconsin, is considered the genotype for that specific location.

Growing medium: sometimes just referred to as medium, this term simply means the mixture that is being used to germinate or grow a particular plant. A growing medium in a greenhouse is usually absent of soil and is instead a sterile mix of products such as vermiculite, perlite and sphagnum peat moss.

Glossary: For Your Understanding

Growing on: a term used by greenhouse growers for the period of time from when a seed germinates, or sprouts, to the time it is ready to be removed from the greenhouse for sale or planting.

Herbaceous: having no woody stems or branches. These plants have green, leafy tissue that dies back in late fall.

Humus: organic matter in an extremely advanced state of decay. In this state of decay, it is ready to be used to amend a garden bed.

Inflorescence: the upper or terminal portion of a plant bearing a cluster of flowers.

Internode: the segment of a stem between two nodes.

Loam: a mixture of sand, silt, and clay. Loam is considered the best soil for growing most crops. Native plant: a plant that was here during colonial times and earlier and that has adapted to the local environment and ecology; present prior to European settlement.

Node: the section on a stem where the leaves and auxillary buds are attached. It is also the potential growing point when doing a stem cutting.

Ovary: the bottom or basil portion of the pistil that will turn into a fruit.

Ovule: an immature seed. The ovule forms after the flower petals have fallen off a flower.

Perennial: a plant that grows two or more years. The tops of perennial wildflowers often die back in winter, but the crown and root system (tuber, tuberous root) remain alive and will spring back to life the following year. Some perennials only live five to six years, but others persist for decades. Most wildflowers are perennial.

Perlite: exploded volcanic ash. It is an ingredient often used in potting mixes in place of sand.

Pistil: the female portion of a flower.

Propagation: to increase the number of plants by sexual (seed) or asexual (cuttings, division) means.

Prairie: an ecosystem made up predominantly of grasses and wildflowers with few woody plants present. There are five classifications of prairies: wet, wet mesic, mesic, dry mesic, and dry.

Rain garden: a garden created to collect runoff from a roof or other source. The main objective of a rain garden is to divert water that can carry pollutants into our water sources.

Savannah: a woodland ecosystem made up of scattered trees or tree colonies interspersed with prairie plants. Oak savannas are the most common savannah in the Midwest.

Scarification: to nick or soak the seed to aid in germination.

Seed coat: the outside covering of a seed.

Separation: a method of propagation used with bulbs and corms where the offspring are pulled away and replanted.

Soil amendment: any organic matter used to enhance the water- and nutrient-retention qualities of the soil.

Sphagnum peat moss: the brown, crumbly organic matter found in a bag of potting soil.

Stamen: the male portion of the plant where pollen is located.

Stratification: a method of chilling seed to mimic the dormant cycle of a seed. The seed is usually in a moist germination medium and is kept in a cool, dark place until it is time to plant.

Vermiculite: a mineral of mica origin that expands when moistened. Used in germination mixes and also to layer on top of seeds to encourage germination.

Wetland: any ecosystem in which the water table is close to the surface or visible for an extended period of time. Wetlands need not have standing water. Wetlands go by different names, including bog, fen, wet prairie, swamp, and marsh.

Wing: a membranous material attached to a seed, in a shape of a wing, that is used to help disperse the seed. Seeds of many conifers have wings.

Woodland: any ecosystem in which trees predominate. Typical woodland communities include beech-sugar maple, oak-hickory, and pine.

APPENDIX A
MORE INFORMATION & RESOURCES

Books/Resources on Propagating Plants

Powell, Eileen. *From Seed to Bloom: How to Grow over 500 Annuals, Perennials & Herbs*. North Adams, MA., 1995.
I've used this book for years when questions arose regarding planting depth, temps, etc.

Protocol Information: Hiawatha National Forest Native Plant Program, USFS.
This work in progress features field notes on propagating plants from the experts working with the U.S. Forest Service.

Smith, Miranda. *The Plant Propagator's Bible*. Emmaus, PA: Rodale Press, 2007.
The book's title says it all.

Information on Building a Rain Garden

Rain Garden Network
Email: info@raingardennetwork.com. Include your name, phone, address (optional) and a short note. We will contact you as soon as possible.
Rain Garden Network can also be reached at:
(773) 774-5333.
www.RainGardenNetwork.com
―――――――――――

Rain Gardens of West Michigan
West Michigan Environmental Action Council
1007 Lake Drive SE
Grand Rapids, Michigan 49506
(616) 454-RAIN or (616) 451-3051, Ext. 29
―――――――――――

On Becoming a Certified Wildlife Habitat

National Wildlife Federation
11100 Wildlife Center Drive
Reston, VA 20190-5362
www.NWF.org
(800) 822-9919 toll-free
―――――――――――

Information on Invasive Species

A Field Identification Guide to Invasive Plants in Michigan's Natural Communities. Michigan State University Extension, 2009.
This invaluable guide to identifying problem plants is the first step to eradication and control. Applicable to states that border Michigan.
―――――――――――

Appendix A

Eastern Upper Peninsula Weed Management Area
EUP CWMA Program Coordinator
Wendy Wagoner
Chippewa/East Mackinac Conservation District
(906) 440-7675
Wendy.Wagoner@MACD.org
www.ChipMackConservation.org/weedmanagement_2.asp

Door County Invasive Species Team (DCIST)
(920) 746-5955 (leave a message!)
dcist1@gmail.com
www.map.co.door.wi.us/swcd/invasive/Publications.htm

Sources for more information on wildflowers and native plants

Michigan Conservation Districts
3001 Coolidge Rd, Suite 250
East Lansing, MI 48823
(517) 324-4421
(517) 324-4435
www.MACD.org
This site links to all of the conservation districts in the state. Invaluable research for all things native, as well as conservation issues.

U.S. Environmental Protection Agency
Great Lakes National Program Office
77 W. Jackson Boulevard (G-17J)
Chicago, Illinois 60604-3511
(312) 353-2117
www.EPA.gov/greenacres
This site is all about landscaping with native plants in the Great Lakes Region.

Wild Ones
PO Box 12
Appleton, WI 54912
National office
(920) 730-3986
(877) FYI-WILD or (877) 394-9453 toll-free
Info@For-Wild.org
www.For-Wild.org
With its roots (pun intended) deeply planted in the Great Lake Region, Wild Ones is one of the premier purveyors of wildflowers in the country with 53 chapters in 12 states.

Michigan Wildflower Association
A rock solid organization that has been promoting the use of wildflowers for decades. It hosts an annual conference.

Sources for wildflower seed and plants

You can obtain a listing of nurseries and companies that supply native seed and plants by contacting the associations and agencies listed below. Some of these companies listed also specialize in wildflower design, installation, maintenance, and even prescribed burns.

Michigan

Michigan Native Plant Producers Association
www.MNPPA.org

Michigan Wildflower Association
www.WildflowersMich.org

Appendix A

Wisconsin

Wisconsin Department of Natural Resources
101 S. Webster Street
PO Box 7921
Madison, Wisconsin 53707-7921
(608) 266-2621
www.DNR.wi.gov

Minnesota

Minnesota Department of Natural Resources
(651) 296-6157
(888) MINN-DNR or (888) 646-6367 toll-free
Info.DNR@state.mn.us
www.DNR.state.mn.us

APPENDIX B
BOOKS, HIKES & MORE

Books on Plant Identification

Brown, Lauren. *Grasses: an Identification Guide*. Boston, New York, London: Houghton Mifflin Company, 1992.
Grasses can be difficult to identify, but are an important cog in the ecological wheel. This book will help you improve your grass ID skills.

Clements, Steven, and Gracie, Carol. Wildflowers in the Field and Forest: A Field Guide to the Northeastern United States. New York: Oxford University Press, 2006.
This detailed guide includes clear photographs of flowering plants and maps that clearly define the geographical range of each flower.

Lund, Harry C. *Michigan Wildflowers*. Holt, MI: Thunder Bay Press, 2004.
This trusted guide includes pictures of wildflowers in bloom with detailed descriptions, making this a good book to turn to for the novice and more seasoned wildflower enthusiast.

McKenny, Margaret, Peterson, Roger Tory. *Wildflowers: Northeastern/North-Central North America* . Boston, MA: Houghton-Mifflin Company, 1979.
Peterson field guides, with accurate botanical drawings throughout, are popular with the novice and advanced naturalist.

Newcomb, Lawrence. *Wildflower Guide*. Boston, New York, London: Little Brown and Company, 1989.
Features a "logical key system" for the person with no botanical training to aid in identififying the many different wildflowers found in the wild.

Rabeler, Richard K. *Gleason's Plants of Michigan*. Ann Arbor, MI: Oakleaf Press, 1998.
An plant identification book for botanists to accurately identify different species of native plants.

Tekiela, Stan. *Wildflowers of Wisconsin*. Cambridge, MN: Adventure Publications, Inc., 2000.
A "user-friendly" guide to indentifying wildflowers in the state of Wisconsin.

Appendix B

Information on Great Places to View Native Plants

Michigan

The Great Waters
www.TheGreatWaters.com
You're bound to find some interesting wildflowers along the hiking trails featured in the map of the Upper Peninsula published by Great Waters. This map belongs in every wildflower lover's glove box or backpack.

Hiawatha National Forest, Upper Peninsula of Michigan
Trails in the Hiawatha: A Guide to Non-Motorized Trails.
Trails, trails and more trails! This little guide book includes a description and directions to some really cool places to observe your favorite wildflowers in the Hiawatha National Forest.

Isle Royale National Park
800 East Lakeshore Drive
Houghton, Michigan 49931-1869
Visitor Information:
(906) 482-0984
www.NPS.gov/isro
A trip to this wilderness park requires some pre-planning. View wildflowers not seen anywhere else, including over 30 orchids.

The Nature Conservancy
Worldwide Office
The Nature Conservancy
4245 North Fairfax Drive, Suite 100
Arlington, VA 22203-1606
(703) 841-5300
www.TNC.org
Find a list of the "Last Great Places" that the conservancy has acquired in the Great Lakes Region, and all over the country, for that matter. Check out their website often; they host guided tours in all states that sometimes include wildflower identification.

North Country Trail Association
229 E. Main Street
Lowell, MI 49331
(616) 897-5987
(866) 445-3628 toll-free
www.NorthCountryTrail.org
This is a trail that traverses the Great Lakes States and on out east. Discover wildflowers along portions of the trail which runs through Minnesota, Wisconsin, Michigan and Ohio.

Pictured Rocks National Lakeshore
P.O. Box 40
Munising, Michigan 49862-0040
Visitor Information: (906) 387-3700
Park Headquarters: (906) 387-2607
www.NPS.gov/piro
Located within the transition zone of the boreal and eastern deciduous forests, this area is prime for viewing unique species of wildflowers. The park features numerous hiking trails and camping facilities, not to mention a newly paved highway that links Munising and Grand Marais, providing a great scenic drive.

Appendix B

Seney Wildlife Refuge
1674 Refuge Entrance Rd.
Seney, MI 49883
(906) 586-9851
www.FWS.gov/midwest/Seney
Besides a vast area of wilderness, which can be hiked, biked or skied, there is also an interpretive center via the main entrance.

Sleeping Bear Dunes National Lakeshore
Sleeping Bear Dunes Visitors Bureau
12 Wood Ridge Road
Glen Arbor, MI 49636
(888) 334-8499 toll-free
Info@SleepingBearDunes.com
www.SleepingBearDunes.com
Discover wildflowers along the dunes and around the inland lakes in this beautiful park. Expect to find spring beauties, columbine, bloodroot, and other common and not-so-common wildflowers.

Woods & Water Ecotours
P.O. Box 114
20 Pickford Ave
Hessel, MI 49745
(906) 484-4157
Info@WoodsWaterEcotours.com
www.WoodsWaterEcotours.com
Guided tours will take you to exotic island destinations where you can view rare wildflowers; hike, bike, or kayak.

Wisconsin

Apostle Islands National Lakeshore
415 Washington Ave
Bayfield, Wisconsin 54814
Headquarters phone
(715) 779-3397
www.NPS.gov/apis
Dubbed the Jewels of the North, this storied national park includes a band of 21 islands and 12 miles of beautiful Lake Superior lakeshore. Over 800 plant species occur within the lakeshore, including Wisconsin State listed endangered and threatened species.

National Parks System
For more information on the different national parks in Wisconsin go to:
www.NPS.gov.

Travel Wisconsin
Wisconsin Department of Tourism
201 West Washington Avenue
PO Box 8690
Madison WI 53708-8690
(608) 266-2161
(800) 432-8747 toll-free
www.TravelWisconsin.com
TourInfo@TravelWisconsin.com
Travel Wisconsin is hosted by the Wisconsin Department of Tourism. This is the go-to place for information on guided wildflower walks throughout the state.

Appendix B

Minnesota

Hiking Trails

As one can imagine, there are many, many hiking trails in the vast wilderness of Minnesota. Some of these range from day trips in and out to guided hikes for the experienced hiker. Wildflowers are in abundance in Minnesota's outback. To find more information on great places to hike and view wildflowers in Minnesota, visit www.trails.com and search for "Minnesota." Happy trails to you!

Minnesota Department of Natural Resources
500 Lafayette Road
St. Paul, MN 55155-4040
(651) 296-6157
(888) 646-6367 toll-free
www.DNR.state.mn.us

You can obtain information on guided wildflower walks in Minnesota, mostly held in the spring of the year (before mosquitoes and black flies become intolerable).

Voyageurs National Park
360 Highway 11 East
International Falls, Minnesota 56649
Park Headquarters
(218) 283-6600
www.NPS.gov/voya

View showy lady's slippers and join the celebration at the Kabetogam's Lady Slipper Festival. While hiking trails abound (nine trails) the park is commonly viewed by boat or kayak.

ABOUT THE AUTHOR

Neil Moran is the author of a popular book on northern gardening called *North Country Gardening: Simple Secrets to Successful Northern Gardening* (Avery Color Studios), and a garden tips booklet called *From Store to Garden: 101 Ways to Make the Most of Garden Store Purchases*. He taught horticulture for several years and continues to speak and hold workshops on gardening and horticulture. He writes garden articles for *Michigan Country Lines* and *Outlook by the Bay*.

Autographed copies of Neil's books can be ordered via:
www.NorthCountryGardening.blogspot.com.

CPSIA information can be obtained at www.ICGtesting.com
Printed in the USA
BVOW080040250512
291057BV00004B/2/P